SAMADHI

Self-Development in Zen, Swordsmanship, and Psychotherapy

MIKE K. SAYAMA

STATE UNIVERSITY OF NEW YORK PRESS

1986

Published by State University of New York Press
© 1986 State University of New York
All rights reserved
Printed in the United States of America
Cover photo of Tanouye Tenshin's hands by Masahiko Wada
Cover and text design by Sushila Blackman
Title page calligraphy of *samadhi* by Omori Sogen

For information, address State University of New York Press,
State University Plaza, Albany, NY 12246

Library of Congress Cataloging in Publication Data
Sayama, Mike K., 1954-
    Samadhi: self development in Zen, swordsmanship,
and psychotherapy.
    (SUNY series in transpersonal and humanistic psychology)
    Bibliography: p.
    Includes index.
    1. Enlightenment (Zen Buddhism) 2. Zen Buddhism —
Psychology. I. Title. II. Series.
BQ9288.S28   1986   294.3'42   85-9894
ISBN: 0-88706-146-x
ISBN 0-88706-147-8 (pbk.)

I dedicate this book to my parents.

I thank Tanouye Roshi for training me these past ten years, my family for their help throughout my life, and Richard Mann and Bill Eastman for the chance to publish this book. I also thank the Institute of Zen Studies for its support during its completion. As I look back across the seven years I have been working on it, I feel grateful to so many friends and relatives that I would not know where to stop if I started thanking all of you individually. Let me then simply place my palms together and bow.

Contents

Preface

The true form of Zen in words would be philosophical poetry. It would be the reflection of existence seeing itself; and like a pristine bell sounding from nowhere to nowhere, it would lead to *samadhi*, the awareness which is itself the wisdom to be realized.

Samadhi is a Sanskrit term identifying an experience which is the key to self development. It can be described as a relaxed concentration in which a person does not freeze because of fear or cling because of desire. In samadhi a person transcends dualism, is fully present moment by moment, and enjoys life to the utmost. At its deepest, samadhi is the experience of interpenetration.

The transpersonal psychology exploring higher levels of consciousness and self-development is just emerging. Its basis is the lives and teachings of the masters of the great spiritual traditions throughout the world. In this book I first focus on a traditional line of Zen Buddhism, presenting six masters in the lineage of Chozen-ji, a Rinzai temple. I then outline a way of self-development based on Zen, swordsmanship, and psychotherapy.

List of Photographs and Illustrations

Interpenetration,
The Buddha's Enlightenment

In human evolution dualism was once our crowning achievement. It distinguished us from animals and gave us the reflective distance to curb blind instinct and superstition, and thus to create culture, science, and the possibility of true freedom. Dualism structures experience into mutually exclusive categories such as subject and object, good and bad, cause and effect, and past, present, and future. These categories have worked so well in ordering nature and people that they are now generally assumed to be real.

Dualism, however, is an ontological error with widespread consequences. It has led us to believe in a universe consisting of independently existing, mechanistically interacting elementary particles. It has led us to identify the Self with an ego in a dying body alienated from the rest of life. It is leading to a world lacking in higher principles and meaning, with people ironically coping with existential anxiety by enhancing egocentric interests at the expense of the more fulfilling common good.

The challenge facing us today is to graduate from dualism and realize that all interpenetrates all without obstruction. Interpenetration is our fundamental experience. Our highest experience is the realization of this experience as fundamental. Thus Shakamuni exclaimed at his enlightenment, "How mysterious, how wonderful! All beings are Buddhas from the beginning."

1

Indian Buddhists conceive of a Universe of infinite time and space in which the creation and dissolution of world systems eternally recur, and sentient beings transmigrate through countless lives on their way to the perfection of a Buddha (The Awakened One). It is said that three incalculable aeons, each longer than 10^{27} years, are needed to become a *bodhisattva* (a being destined to become a Buddha), and another one hundred aeons to fulfill this destiny. Shakamuni is the historical Buddha of the present world system.

He was born as an Indian prince over twenty-five hundred years ago. At birth it was foretold that he would be a great king or a religious prophet. The king wanted his son to succeed him and kept Shakamuni away from any suffering which might lead to spiritual searching. Growing up within the palace walls, he excelled in all the martial and cultural arts, married the most beautiful woman in the kingdom, fathered a son, and enjoyed the best that the material world had to give.

At twenty-nine, however, he ventured outside the palace and was confronted by old age, disease, death, and poverty. The impermanence of existence transformed his happiness into anguish, and he felt like a man trapped in a burning house. Renouncing his family and kingdom, he sought salvation through ascetic practice.

For six years he practiced austerities that brought him to the brink of death, until finally he sat in the lotus position with the vow not to move until he was enlightened. He exhausted his intellect going over and over the twelvefold chain of causation in the endless wheel of suffering. Eventually he entered into the deepest of samadhis. On the morning of the seventh day, the twinkling of a star shattered his samadhi and awakened him.

After his enlightenment he first taught that all things and events in the universe interpenetrate each other freely without obstruction. But when no one could follow him, he taught the Four Noble Truths instead. The principle of interpenetration has been elaborated in the Kegon Sutra in a four-fold conception of existence:

1. The world viewed as individual existences.
2. The world viewed as absolute.
3. The world conceived as individuals retaining their individuality in the absolute.
4. The world conceived as each revealed through each other, so that each individual has no hindrance from being merged in every other.[1]

D.T. Suzuki called the principle of interpenetration the culmination of Buddhist philosophy. It is illustrated by the metaphor of mirrors encircling a candle. The candlelight reflects itself in every mirror, and every reflection is again reflected in every mirror such that a perfect interplay of lights is reflected into infinity.

Interpenetration is the transcendental oneness which is at the heart of the teachings of sages throughout history. For example:

> There is neither seer nor seeing nor seen. There is but one Reality. It is changeless, formless and absolute. How can it be divided?
>
> There is but one Reality—like a brimming ocean in which all appearances are dissolved. It is changeless, formless, and absolute. How can it be divided? . . .
>
> It is our delusion which superimposes the universe of differences upon Brahman. But the wise know that this universe has no separate reality. It is identical with Brahman, its ground. . . .
>
> This delusion of difference has its origin in the gross mind. When the mind is transcended, it ceases. Therefore let your mind be absorbed in contemplation of the Atman, the Reality, your inmost essence.
>
> —Shankara[2]

> When is a man in mere understanding? I answer, "When a man sees one thing as separated from another." And when is a man above mere understanding? That I can tell you, "When a man sees All in all, then a man stands beyond mere understanding."
>
> —Eckhart[3]

> Each being contains in itself the whole intelligible world. Therefore All is everywhere. Each is there All, and All is each. Man as he now is has ceased to be the All. But when he ceases to be an individual, he raises himself again and penetrates the whole world.
>
> —Plotinus[4]

Without the illuminating presence of such individuals, however, interpenetration could be too easily dismissed before as esotericism. But now following the logic of dualism to the nth degree, paradoxically, physics also points to the fundamental oneness of the universe. The analysis of subatomic and astrophysical phenomena refutes the dualistic, mechanistic paradigm of the universe and opens the mind to new possibilities. It has led eminent physicists to such thoughts as follow:

A human being is a part of the whole, called by us "Universe"; a part limited in time and space. He experiences himself, his thoughts and feelings as something separated from the rest—a kind of optical delusion of his consciousness. This delusion is a kind of a prison for us, restricting us to our personal desires and to affection for a few persons nearest us. Our task must be to free ourselves from this prison.

—Albert Einstein[5]

It had not been possible to see what could be wrong with the fundamental concepts like matter, space, time, and causality that had been so extremely successful in the history of science. Only experimental research itself, carried out with all the refined equipment that technical science could offer. . . provided the basis for a critical analysis—or, one may say, enforced the critical analysis—of the concepts, and finally resulted in the dissolution of the rigid frame.

—Werner Heisenberg[6]

Subject and object are only one. The barrier between them cannot be said to have broken down as a result of recent experience in the physical sciences, *for this barrier does not exist.*

—Ernest Schroedinger[7]

Inconceivable as it seems to ordinary reason, you—and all other conscious beings as such—are all in all. Hence this life of yours which you are living is not merely a piece of the entire existence, but is in a certain sense the *whole*. . . . Thus you can throw yourself flat on the ground, stretched out upon Mother Earth, with the certain conviction that you are one with her and she with you. You are as firmly established, as invulnerable as she, indeed a thousand times firmer and more invulnerable. As surely as she will engulf you tomorrow, so surely will she bring you forth anew to new striving and suffering. And not merely "some day":

Now, today, every day she is bringing you forth, not *once* but thousands upon thousands of times, just as every day she engulfs you a thousand times over.

—Ernest Schroedinger[8]

Although the new physics begins to sound like philosophical mysticism, they are not the same. The wisdom of the sages is a direct expression of the absolute transcending all forms, including those of physics. It expresses the absolute which cannot be named. Einstein said:

> The most beautiful emotion we can experience is the mystical. It is the sower of all true art and science. He to whom this emotion is a stranger. . . is as good as dead. To know that what is impenetrable to us really exists, manifesting itself as the highest wisdom and the most radiant beauty, which our dull faculties can comprehend only in their most primitive forms—this knowledge, this feeling, is at the center of true religiousness. In this sense only I belong to the ranks of devoutly religious men.[9]

The growing convergence between scientific findings and the insights of sages does, however, signal a revolutionary shift from a dualistic to a wholistic paradigm. As our knowledge increases, it will become clearer that our highest ideals are grounded in the actual nature of the universe. It will become clearer that effectiveness and creativeness in any field ultimately come from self-development. The new physics can help to shatter the dualistic perspective and the limitations it places on human potential, for it depicts a reality where there is no such thing as a thing, where all is interpenetrating fields of energy in flux; where space, time, and causality disappear. Consider the following phenomena: 1. An electron jumps from one position to another without passing through any positions in between. 2. Two atoms which initially combined to form a molecule are separated by a great distance. When a change in one occurs, a change in the other simultaneously occurs.

To make sense of such phenomena the physicist David Bohm proposes the holomovement, a model of "the unbroken wholeness of the totality of existence as an undivided flowing movement without borders." In the holomovement particles no matter how small are the manifestation on the explicate order of patterns enfolded in the implicate order, which is the more fundamental level of reality. Bohm offers the following mechanical analogies to illustrate how his model accounts for the phenomena described above.

To account for electrons skipping spaces, he gives the example of a device consisting of two concentric glass cylinders with a thick fluid between them. A drop of insoluble ink, A, is placed in the liquid, and the outer cylinder is turned so that the ink drop is drawn out into a fine thread that eventually becomes invisible. Another drop, B, is inserted in a different position, and is also enfolded into the liquid. After enfolding a large number of drops along the line AB, the cylinder is rotated rapidly in the reverse direction such that what is seen is apparently a particle crossing space. Bohm comments:

> Such enfoldment and unfoldment in the implicate order may evidently provide a new model of, for example, an electron which is quite different from that provided by the current mechanistic notion of a particle that exists at each moment only in a small region of space and that changes its position continuously with time. What is essential to this new model is that the electron is instead to be understood through a total set of enfolded ensembles, which are generally not localized in space. At any given moment one of these may be unfolded and therefore localized, but in the next moment, this one enfolds to be replaced by the one that follows. The notion of continuity of existence is approximated by that of very rapid recurrence of similar forms, changing in a simple and regular way. . . . More fundamentally, the particle is only an abstraction that is manifest to our senses. *What is* is always a totality of ensembles, all present together, in an orderly series of stages of enfoldment and unfoldment, which intermingle and interpenetrate throughout the whole of space.[10]

To account for instantaneous, corresponding changes in distant objects, he uses the analogy of two television cameras focused on fish swimming in an aquarium. The cameras are at right angles to each other and transmit different but correlated images of fishes swimming in the tank to two television screens in another room. Clearly neither image causes related changes in the other. Both are two-dimensional projections of a more fundamental, three-dimensional reality. Similarly the simultaneous, correlated changes of the two atoms described earlier must be viewed as a projection of change occurring at a more fundamental, multidimensional level of reality.

> Quite generally, then, the implicate order has to be extended into a multidimensional reality. In principle this reality is one unbroken whole, including the entire universe with all its 'fields' and 'particles'. Thus we have to say that the holomovement enfolds and unfolds in a multidimensional order, the dimensionality of which is effectively infinite. However, as we have already seen, relatively independent sub-totalities can be generally abstracted, which may be approximated as autonomous.[11]

In Bohm's model the electron is not a particle that dematerializes and rematerializes from place to place; nor does information travel faster than the speed of light from one atom to another. It is more accurate to say that the electron is always already there and that information is everywhere in the enfolded patterns of the implicate order.

The new physics refutes the dualistic paradigm, but it is not enough to know this intellectually. A person must experience the unbroken, flowing wholeness of the universe and live accordingly. This requires the cultivation of samadhi until consciousness transcends dualism. It is possible to cultivate samadhi through the perfection of the forms of any field of endeavor. Concentrated and refined effort naturally leads to the absorption of subject into object. But such a samadhi is limited to the specific field. The great spiritual traditions, however, developed ways of mind-body training which transformed the structure of being and enabled a person to abide in samadhi while living fully in the relative world. Such a person has gone beyond the suffering inherent in dualism and lives a bright and boundless life like the smiling sage who mingles among people with fish, wine, and bliss-bestowing hands.

The first part of this book studies self-realization in the tradition of Zen Buddhism. The essence of Zen is the Buddha's enlightenment. Historically it is one of the schools of Mahayana Buddhism, originating in the sixth century from a blending of the metaphysics of Indian Buddhism with the pragmatism of Chinese Taoism. Bodhidharma, the First Patriarch of Zen in China, characterized it as:

> *A special transmission outside the scriptures,*
> *Not dependent on words and letters,*
> *Direct pointing at the essence of human being,*
> *Seeing into one's nature and becoming a Buddha.*[12]

In the literature of Zen, samadhi refers to both the highest state of awareness and the means to this state. Master Shibayama Zenkei defined samadhi as follows:

> Originally a Sanskrit word meaning to concentrate one's mind on one point so that the mind remains still and quiet. In Zen, samadhi is used in a somewhat different sense, that is, it is the pure working of no-mind that has transcended both action and quietude.[13]

From the perspective of training samadhi is a state of pure and relaxed concentration which is strengthened and refined by rigorous psychophysical discipline. In samadhi awareness is clear and unhindered by preconceptions and preferences, and one experiences the interpenetration of all things as emptiness. A distinction, however, remains between emptiness and the suchness of the relative world, between samadhi and ordinary mind. When samadhi deepens and is finally shattered, there is true enlightenment transcending every trace of duality. But the formulation of training leading to samadhi, and samadhi to enlightenment is misleading. From a higher perspective, as Master Dogen said, training is enlightenment, and enlightenment is training.

Around the eleventh century various schools of Zen were transmitted from China to Japan. The two major remaining schools in Japan, the Soto and the Rinzai, are described below by a contemporary master of each.

> This is the real life, when practice and realization are one. Finally he reaches the ultimate goal of Zen, to adapt freely to the world. Now the parents are like parents, the children like children, the husband like a husband, and the wife like a wife. The willow is green and the flower is red. . . . We call it ordinary life, and it is, but this is also the Truth unchanged throughout the ages. See! When it is cold the bird perches on the tree; the duck takes to water. Each repairs to its own refuge. The truth is the truth in each. Neither is better—there is no better or worse because there is no inequality. Where there is no inequality, the heart is tranquil and the world radiates the light of peace. This is our Soto Zen, and it is the final resting place of Zen.
>
> —Takashina Rosen[14]

> Now as to the characteristics of the Rinzai Sect, we read. . . as follows: "The great spirit of Zen, leaping out of the basket or out of the nest in its vigorous operation, dances about like a tiger, leaps like a dragon, flies like a star, roars like thunder, opens and closes the Gate of Heaven, turns the Earth on its axis, displays its high spirits to the extent of pushing up Heaven, and goes beyond the dualities of rolling and unfolding, catching and freeing, and killing and reviving in the exceptional Way." The above expressions are difficult to understand, but at any rate, these inspiring words seem to help me vividly visualize the activ-

ity of the spirit of Zen in all its inviolable freedom and vitality, almost to the extent of upsetting Heaven and Earth.

—Omori Sogen[15]

Both Rinzai and Soto schools are currently being transmitted to America through various lines. The first part of the book presents the tradition of Zen through the lives and teachings of six masters in a traditional line of Rinzai Zen: Bodhidharma, Hui-neng, Lin-chi, Hakuin, Omori, and Tanouye. They are masters in the line of Chozen-ji, a temple in Hawaii established by Omori Sogen in 1972.

The second part of the book presents Zen therapy, a way of transpersonal development emphasizing the cultivation of samadhi through psychophysical training. It is a way based on theories and practices from Zen, the martial arts, and psychotherapy. While transforming insights may occur in an instant, development is a process which takes time and energy as new cognitive structures must emerge and the body must be freed from unnatural habits. Otherwise, insights will be just passing highs, and a person will quickly regress to egotistical patterns under stress.

"Transpersonal" refers to the highest level of self-development. At this level a person transcends the identification with the ego and the dualistic structure of ordinary experience. One of the forerunners of transpersonal psychology was Carl Jung. He anticipated the convergence of physics and psychology, identified the collective unconscious, and coined the term *synchronicity* as an acausal connecting principle. He wrote:

> Sooner or later, nuclear physics and the psychology of the unconscious will draw closer together as both of them, independently of one another and from opposite directions, push forward into transcendental territory. . . . Psyche cannot be totally different from matter, for how otherwise could it move matter? And matter cannot be alien to psyche, for how else could matter produce psyche? Psyche and matter exist in the same world, and each partakes of the other, otherwise any reciprocal action would be impossible. If research could only advance far enough, we should arrive at an ultimate agreement between physical and psychological concepts. Our present attempts may be bold, but I believe they are on the right lines.[16]

Jung made extensive studies of the myths and symbols across cultures and found striking similarities which led him to the collective unconscious. The collective unconscious contains the archetypes, the primordial images and experiences imprinted on the human psyche in the course of phylogenesis and expressed in myths and symbols. He wrote:

> I can only gaze with wonder and awe at the depths and heights of our psychic nature. Its non-spatial universe conceals an untold abundance of images which have accumulated over millions of years of living development and become fixed in the organism. My consciousness is like an eye that penetrates the most distant spaces, yet it is the psychic non-ego that fills them with non-spatial images. . . . Besides this picture I would like to place the spectacle of the starry heavens at night, for the only equivalent of the universe within is the universe without.[17]

Buddhist metapsychology goes beyond the collective unconscious and postulates the storehouse unconscious which contains the images of cosmogenesis. Beyond the storehouse unconscious is the transcendent Unconscious which is beyond the duality of conscious and unconscious.

Jung also acknowledged meaningful, acausal relationships which he termed synchronicity and gave the following event as an example.

> A young woman patient, in spite of efforts made on both sides, proved to be psychologically inaccessible. The difficulty lay in the fact that she always knew better about everything. Her excellent education had provided her with a weapon ideally suited to this purpose, namely a highly polished Cartesian rationalism with an impeccably "geometrical" idea of reality. After several fruitless attempts to sweeten her rationalism with a somewhat more human understanding, I had to confine myself to the hope that something unexpected and irrational would turn up, something that would burst the intellectual retort into which she had sealed herself. Well, I was sitting opposite her one day, with my back to the window, listening to her flow of rhetoric. She had had an impressive dream the night before, in which someone had given her a golden scarab—a costly piece of jewelry. While she was still telling me this dream, I heard something behind me gently tapping on the window. I turned round and saw that it was a fairly large flying insect that was knocking against the window pane from outside in the obvious effort to get into the darkened room. This seemed to me very strange. I opened the window immediately and caught the insect in the air

as it flew in. It was a scarabaeid beetle. . . whose gold-green
color most nearly resembles that of a golden scarab. I handed
the beetle to my patient with the words, "Here is your scarab."
This experience punctured the desired hole in her rationalism
and broke the ice of her intellectual resistance.[18]

In this example, Jung, the patient, the dream, and the beetle are all
the play of one mind. Jung was effective synchronistically at the
implicate order of reality. In Taoist terms, abiding in Tao, he did
nothing and nothing was left undone.

Like quantum phenomena in physics, the collective unconscious
and synchronicity jar the common assumptions of the nature of ourselves and reality. But in psychology it was not until the humanistic
movement of the 1960's that the transcendental aspects of the self
received serious consideration in the work of Abraham Maslow,
who developed a hierarchy of needs ranging from the physiological,
to the interpersonal, to the existential. Transpersonal psychology is
the fourth psychology predicted by Maslow in 1968:

> I consider Humanistic, Third Force Psychology to be transi-
> tional, a preparation for a still "higher" Fourth Psychology,
> transpersonal, transhuman, centered in the cosmos rather than
> in human needs and interests, going beyond humanness, identity,
> self-actualization, and the like. . . . Without the transcendent
> and the transpersonal, we get sick, violent, and nihilistic, or else
> hopeless and apathetic. We need something "bigger than we are"
> to be awed by and to commit ourselves to in a new, naturalistic,
> empirical, non-churchly sense, perhaps as Thoreau and Whitman,
> William James and John Dewey did.[19]

Richard Mann defines the field of transpersonal psychology well
in his study of Siddha Yoga.

> Transpersonal psychology, as I see it, is defined by the pri-
> mary place it gives to the concept of the absolute in its analysis
> of human life. This commitment to honoring the reality of the
> absolute should not be confused with a commitment to any spe-
> cific imagery, formulation, or spiritual practice. Transpersonal
> psychology will perform a much needed function if it serves all
> the diverse systems of worship and scriptural narrative by provid-
> ing each a place within its perimeter. If it can develop analytic
> categories that permit us to see the commonalities as well as the

differences among the many ways of approaching the absolute, it will have greatly enriched the human community. . . .

The place to start is with the absolute. Whereas scientific and clinical psychology deliberately and, it could be argued, wisely limit their concepts to what I label the relative domain, transpersonal psychology conceives of a reality that includes both relative and absolute. We shall see whether this two-category model of reality is transpersonal psychology's final word on the subject. For a start, however, there is no more essential assertion than that reality includes more than the temporary, conditional, causal universe. . . . It may be that the paradigm guiding our conception of physical and psychic reality is limiting our understanding of the role of the absolute in our daily lives. Only after reformulating our fundamental assumptions concerning observable reality can we develop a transpersonal psychology that appreciates both being and becoming, both the unchanging and the endless processes of transformation.[20]

The fundamental tenet of transpersonal psychology is that the universe is one mind evolving to see itself. This seeing is the fundamental drive of life. In human being life has developed the neurolinguistic sophistication needed for self-reflection. After countless generations, the ego has finally become a phylogenetic legacy for modern human being. The task before us is no longer to differentiate from nature and develop the ego, but transcend the ego and realize the true Self that is one with the universe. Human destiny is fulfilled in this experience of existence seeing itself. Jung put it this way:

"But why on earth," you may ask, "should it be necessary for man to achieve, by hook or crook, a higher level of consciousness?" This is truly the crucial question, and I do not find the answer easy. Instead of a real answer, I can only make a confession of faith: I believe that, after thousands and millions of years, someone had to realize that this wonderful world of mountains and oceans, suns and moons, galaxies and nebulae, plants and animals *exists*. From a low hill in the Ahti plains of East Africa I once watched the vast herds of wild animals grazing in soundless stillness, as they had done from time immemorial, touched only by the breath of a primeval world. I felt then as if I were the first man, the first creature, to know that all this *is*. The entire world around me was still in its primeval state; it did not know that it *was*. And then, in that one moment in which I came to know, the world sprang into being; without that moment it would never have been. All Nature seeks this goal and finds it fulfilled in man, but only in the most highly developed and most fully conscious man.[21]

Today dualistic, linear thinking has turned full circle to confirm oneness as the fundamental reality. Seamless because infinitely differentiated, brimming with creativity because empty, interpenetrating because transcendent, this reality is your true Self.

CHOZEN-JI
LINE

It is said that the teachings are transmitted from mind-to-mind from one master to another, like a line of pure consciousness streaming across the centuries.

China

Bodhidharma
Hui-ke
Seng-ts'an
Tao-shin
Hung-jen
Hui-neng Ta-chien
Nan-yueh Huai-jang
Ma-tsu Tao-i
Po-chang Huai-hai
Huang-po Hsi-yun
Lin-chi Yi-hsuan
Hsing-hua Ts'un-chieng
Nan-yuan Hui-yu
Feng-hsueh Yen-chao
Shou-shan Sheng-nien
Fun'yo Zensho
Shi-shuang Ch'u-yuan
Yang-chih Fang-hui
Po-yun Shou-tuan
Wu-tsu Fa-yen
Yuan-wu K'o-ch'in
Hu-ch'iu Shao-lung
Ying-an T'an-hua
Mi-an Hsien-chieh
Sung-yuan Ch'ung-yueh
Yun-an Pu-yen
Hsu-t'ang Chih-yu

Japan

Nampo Shomyo

Shuho Myocho

Kanzan Egen

Jyuo Soshitsu

Muin Soin

Nippo Soshun

Giten Gensho

Sekko Soshin

Toyo Eicho

Taiga Tankyo

Koho Genkun

Sensho Zuicho

Ian Chisatsu

Tozen Soshin

Yozan Keiyo

Gudo Toshoku

Shido Bunan

Dokyo Etan

Hakuin Ekaku

Gasan Jito

Inzan Itan

Taigen Shigen

Gisan Zenrai

Tekisui Giboku

Ryoen Genseki

Seisetsu Genjyo

America

Omori Sogen

Tanouye Tenshin

Bodhidharma

Several hundred years after the Buddha's death, over twenty
schools claimed orthodoxy. Eventually two major schools emerged:
the Theravada (the Teachings of the Elders) and the Mahayana (the
Great Vehicle). The Theravada School was conservative and emphasized ethics and personal salvation. The Mahayana School was more
progressive and emphasized metaphysics and universal enlightenment in the ideal of the Bodhisattva who vowed not to enter Nirvana until all sentient beings were saved. Zen emerged as a distinctive school from the blending of Mahayana metaphysics with Taoist
pragmatism five generations after Bodhidharma transmitted the
essence of Buddhism to China in 520 A.D.

Tao is the Chinese term for the absolute. It is a poetic term layered
with meanings. Etymologically the character for Tao consists of
symbols representing a path, a human head, and a foot. It can be
interpreted most simply as a path for people to follow. Tao is not a
metaphysical abstraction but the fundamental rhythm, flow, and
force of the universe. Lao Tzu wrote:

Tao is real, yet unnameable.
It is original non-differentiation and invisible.
Nevertheless, nothing in the universe can dominate it.
If rulers and lords were able to abide with it, all
*   things in the universe would yield to them*
*   naturally.*

Heaven and earth are unified and rain the dew of peace.
Without being ordered to do so, people become
  harmonious by themselves.
When discrimination begins, names arise.
After names arise, one should know where to abide.
When one knows where to abide, one is never exhausted.
To abide with Tao in the world is to be the same as
  mountain streams flowing to the rivers and to the
  sea.[1]

Bodhidharma described enlightenment as entering the Tao. Little is known about his background except that he was the third son of a king and succeeded Hannyatara, the thirty-fourth Indian patriarch. Among the illustrious figures of his line were Asvagosha, author of *The Awakening of Faith*, and Nagarjuna, one of the greatest Indian philosophers. In his old age Bodhidharma made the long journey to China. He wrote:

The original reason of my coming to this country
Was to transmit the Law in order to save the confused;
One flower with five petals is unfolded,
And the bearing of fruit will come by itself.[2]

His meeting with Emperor Wu is a classic story. The Emperor asked Bodhidharma, "I have built temples, copied sacred books, and supported monks and nuns. What do you think my merit might be?"

"None whatever!" Bodhidharma bluntly replied.

"Why?" demanded the astonished Emperor.

Bodhidharma replied, "These are inferior deeds which will cause you to be born in the heavens or on this earth again. They still show traces of worldliness. Like shadows following objects, they only seem to exist. A true meritorious deed is full of pure wisdom; it is perfect and mysterious. Its real nature is beyond the grasp of human intelligence. It is not to be sought after through worldly achievement."

The Emperor then asked, "What is the first principle of the holy doctrine?"

"Vast emptiness, no holiness," replied Bodhidharma.

"Who is it then that is now confronting me?" asked the Emperor.

"No knowing," said Bodhidharma and left.[3]

The Emperor with his primitive notions of Buddhism as a religion of salvation through the accumulation of merit from good deeds was unable to understand Bodhidharma. Seeing that the times were not ready for Zen, Bodhidharma crossed the Yang-tse River. It is said that he crossed standing on a reed. This image is a favorite among Zen painters and symbolizes the exquisitely balanced state of the master riding out the waves of karma. Meanwhile the Emperor recounted the interview to his advisor who exclaimed that Bodhidharma had brought the true teachings of Buddhism to China. The Emperor was dismayed and wanted to call Bodhidharma back, but the advisor said Bodhidharma would not turn back.

Bodhidharma went to the Shaolin Temple where he spent all his time sitting facing the wall in meditation. A monk named Hui-ke, already middle-aged and very learned, came day and night begging for instruction. But Bodhidharma simply continued sitting.

Finally one evening Hui-ke stood erect and unmoving through a heavy snowfall which reached above his knees toward daybreak.

Bodhidharma pitied him and said, "You have been standing long in the snow. What are you seeking?"

Hui-ke said, "I beg you, Master, with your compassion open your gate of Dharma (Truth, the principle of the universe) and save all of us beings."

Bodhidharma said, "The incomparable Truth of the Buddhas can only be attained by eternally striving, practicing what cannot be practiced and bearing the unbearable. How can you, with your little virtue, little wisdom, and with your easy and self-conceited mind, dare to aspire to attain the true teaching. It is only so much labor lost."

Listening to Bodhidharma's admonition, Hui-ke secretly took his knife and cut off his left arm. Bodhidharma recognized his Dharma caliber and accepted him.

Hui-ke asked, "Is it possible to listen to Buddha Dharma?"

Bodhidharma replied, "The Buddha Dharma cannot be attained by following others."

Hui-ke said, "My mind is not yet at peace. I beg you, Master, please give it peace."

Bodhidharma said, "Bring it here, and I will pacify it."

Hui-ke hesitated for a moment but finally said, "I have sought it these many years, and still I cannot get hold of it!"

Bodhidharma said, "There! It is pacified once and for all."[4]

Bodhidharma stayed nine years facing the wall at the Shaolin Temple.

When he taught Hui-ke, it was only in the following way: "Externally keep yourself away from all relationships, and inter-

nally have no cravings in your heart. When your mind is like a
straight-standing wall, you may enter the Tao.". . .
     One day Hui-ke said, "I know how to keep myself from all
relationships."
     "You make it a total annihilation, do you not?"
     "No, Master, I do not."
     "How do you testify to your realization?"
     "I know it always in a most intelligible way, but to express it
in words — that is impossible."
     Bodhidharma responded, "That is the mind-essence itself
transmitted by all the Buddhas. Harbour no doubts about it."[5]

Bodhidharma eventually designated Hui-ke as the Second Chinese Patriarch and presented him with his robe and bowl as symbols
of the Dharma transmission and *The Lankavatara Sutra* as "the
essential teachings of the Buddha concerning his mental ground."
     Nothing is known about Bodhidharma's death, but it was widely
rumored that he was over a hundred and fifty years old. Suzuki writes
that his originality can be seen in his substitution of *pi* (wall) for
chueh (enlightenment) to describe meditation as wall-contemplation
rather than enlightenment-contemplation.

It was so concrete, so graphic; there was nothing abstract and
conceptual about it. . . . The underlying meaning of "wall contemplation" must be found in the subjective condition of a Zen
master, which is highly concentrated and rigidly exclusive of all
ideas and sensuous images.[6]

By sitting nine years facing the wall, Bodhidharma successfully
transmitted Zen to China and definitively established zazen as the
basic practice which sustains the line to this day. Below is his trea-
tise on "The Twofold Entrance to Tao."

THE TWOFOLD ENTRANCE TO TAO

There are many entrances to Tao, but they are of two sorts
only: entrance by higher intuition and entrance by practical living.
     The True Nature is the same in all sentient beings. The rea-
son it does not manifest itself is due to the overwrapping of
external objects and false thoughts. When a man abandons the
false and embraces the true and in singleness of thought prac-

tices wall-contemplation, he finds that there is neither self nor other and that the masses and the worthies are of one essence. . . . He will no longer be a slave to words for he is in silent communion with Tao itself. Free from conceptual discrimination, he is serene and non-acting. This is called entrance by higher intuition.

Entrance by practical living consists of the four acts in which all other acts are included: 1. To know how to requite hatred. 2. To be obedient to karma. 3. Not to crave anything. 4. To accord with Dharma.

1. What is meant by how to requite hatred? He who disciplines himself in the Tao should think thus when he has to struggle with adversity: "During innumerable past ages I have wandered through a multiplicity of existences, all the while giving myself to unimportant details of life at the expense of the essentials thus creating infinite occasions for hate, ill will, and wrong doing. The fruits of past evil deeds are to be gathered now. Neither gods nor men can foretell what is coming upon me. I will submit myself willingly and patiently to all, and I will never complain. The Sutra teaches me not to worry over bad fortune because when things are surveyed by a higher intelligence, the foundation of causation is reached." When this thought is awakened in a man, he will be in accord with Reason because he makes the best use of hatred and turns it to the service of his advance to Tao.

2. Obedience to karma means this: There is no self in whatever beings are produced by the interplay of karmic conditions. The pleasure I experience is also the result of my previous action. action. If I am rewarded with fortune, honor, and so on, this is the outcome of my past deeds which by reason of causation affect my present life. When the force of karma is exhausted, the result I am enjoying now will disappear. What is then the use of being joyful over it? Gain or loss, let me accept the karma as it brings me the one or the other. The Mind itself knows neither increase nor decrease. The wind of pleasure and pain will not stir me for I am silently in harmony with Tao. . . .

3. Not craving anything means this: In eternal confusion men of the world are attached everywhere to one thing or another. This is called craving. The wise, however, understand the truth, and their minds abide serenely in the uncreated while their bodies move about according to the laws of causation. All things are empty and there is nothing desirable to seek after.

Where there is the merit of brightness, there surely lurks the demerit of darkness. This triple world where we stay altogether too long is like a house on fire. All that has a body suffers, and nobody really knows what peace is. Because the wise are thoroughly acquainted with this truth, they are never attached to things that change; their thoughts are quieted; they never crave anything. . . .

4. Being in accord with Dharma means this: The Reason we call the Dharma in its essence is pure. It is the principle of emptiness in all that is manifested. It is above defilements and attachments, and there is no self, no other in it. . . . In the Dharma there is no desire to possess, therefore, the wise are ever ready to practice charity with their body, life, and property; they never begrudge; and they never know what an ill grace means. As they have a perfect understanding of the threefold nature of emptiness, they are above partialities and attachment. Only because of their will to cleanse all beings of their stains, they come among them as of them, but they are not attached to form. This is the self-benefitting phase of their lives. They also know, however, how to benefit others and again how to glorify the truth of enlightenment. As with the virtue of charity, so with the other five virtues. The wise practice the six virtues of perfection (charity, morality, patience, perseverance, meditation, and wisdom) to get rid of confused thoughts, and yet they are not conscious of engaging in any meritorious deeds. This is called being in accord with Dharma.[7]

Hui-neng Ta-chien

After succeeding Bodhidharma, Hui-ke lived unassumingly among the peasants. But his teachings were so inspirational that in the end he incurred the jealousy of the clergy, who accused him of heresy. Condemned to death at a hundred and seven, Hui-ke submitted composedly, saying that it was an old karmic debt. He was succeeded by Seng-ts'an, author of an important text called "Inscribed on the Believing Mind." Next came Tao-hsin, who performed miracles and began the monastic tradition in Zen. Then came Hung-jen, the teacher of Hui-neng. With Hui-neng, the Sixth Patriarch, all five petals of the flower of Zen in China were unfolded, and Bodhidharma's prophecy fulfilled.

Hui-neng was born in 638 in South China into a very poor family.[1] His father died when he was still a child, and Hui-neng supported himself and his mother by selling firewood. One day while delivering some wood, he happened to hear someone chanting the *Diamond Sutra*. The passage "No mind, no abode, and here works the mind" triggered an insight in him. Learning that the sutra came from Master Hung-jen, Hui-neng set his mind on seeing him. In the course of time a man gave him money he could leave for the care of his mother, and he set out.

After a long, hard journey, Hui-neng arrived at the monastery. He was twenty-four, insignificant, and shabby. Master Hung-jen asked him, "Where do you come from?" Hui-neng replied, "From Ling-nan, Master." "What are you seeking?" asked Hung-jen. "I want to become a Buddha," said Hui-neng. "You monkeys of Ling-nan do not have the Buddha Nature. How can you expect to become a Buddha!" replied Hung-jen. Hui-neng responded, "There is a distinction of south and north for man, but how can there be such a distinction for Buddha Nature." Hung-jen recognized Hui-neng's potential and allowed him to stay as a lay brother assigned to cleaning rice. Eight months passed with Hui-neng silently concentrating on his discipline.

Then one day Master Hung-jen told his disciples, "Each of you make a poem to show your realization. Demonstrate your Zen ability and show whether you are ready to be the Dharma successor." Shen-hsiu, the head monk who was much respected by all, wrote the following on a wall:

> *The body is the Bodhi-tree.*
> *The mind is like a bright mirror.*
> *Moment by moment wipe it carefully,*
> *Never letting dust collect.*

Hung-jen publicly commended the verse as a guide to practice but privately told Shen-hsiu that he had not yet reached true understanding and encouraged him on. But after several days Shen-hsiu remained unable to write another poem. Meanwhile Hui-neng overheard Shen-hsiu's poem being recited by a monk, saw that it did not hit the mark, and so made a poem himself. Being illiterate he asked a monk to write it next to Shen-hsiu's.

> *There is no Bodhi-tree,*
> *Nor mind of mirror bright.*
> *Since from the first not a thing is,*
> *Where can dust alight?*

Shen-hsiu's poem separates the mind and the one who perceives and maintains its purity. By conscientiously eliminating rising thoughts and feelings and disengaging experience from categories and cravings, a pure but static state is attained. This practice makes spiritual training into a logical consciously-directed process of acquisition. By binding one to purity rather than freeing one from all forms, it kills rather than enhances life. In contrast Hui-neng's poem negates all forms, points directly to Emptiness, and leaves no foothold for dualistic interpretation.

Hung-jen recognized the transcendental quality of Hui-neng's poem but thought that as a young, nameless lay brother he would not be accepted by the monks. So in secret at night Hung-jen expounded *The Diamond Sutra* to Hui-neng who was immediately awakened. Hung-jen gave him Bodhidharma's robe as proof of the transmission and instructed him to hide and deepen himself until the times were right for his teachings.

Hui-neng left the monastery but was pursued by a group of monks. Among them was Ming, a straightforward, sharp-tempered man who had been a general before becoming a monk in middle age. After all others had given up, he finally caught up to Hui-neng on a mountain pass.

Hui-neng saw him coming, laid the robe on a stone, and said, "This robe symbolizes faith in the Dharma transmission. How can it be fought for by force? If you dare take it by violence, do as you like." Ming tried to pick up the robe, but it was as immovable as a mountain. Terrified, he implored Hui-neng, "I have come for the Dharma, not for the robe. I beg you, please teach me, lay brother!" Hui-neng said, "Think neither good nor evil. At that moment what is the true Self of Monk Ming?" Ming was at once enlightened. Dripping with sweat, he shed tears of gratitude, bowed reverently, and asked, "Besides these secret words and meanings, is there any further instruction?" Hui-neng said, "What I have told you is not secret. If you are truly awakened to your Original Nature, everything you see, everything you hear is nothing but 'it.' What else can there be? If you think there is some secret, it is of your own making."

In his encounter with Hui-neng, Ming put his conception of himself and his world to a decisive test. Because he was utterly committed to safeguarding the sanctity of Zen by recovering Bodhidharma's robe, his reality collapsed when he could not lift it. Master Shibayama wrote, "Hesitating and trembling, he simply stood there, petrified. This unexpected spiritual impulse must have thrown the sincere and forthright Ming into the bottomless abyss of the Great Doubt. His ego-centered and enraged self was at once completely smashed." Completely defenseless, Ming then threw his whole being at Hui-neng's feet and begged for instruction. Cuttingly asking, "Think neither good nor evil, what is the true Self of Monk Ming?" Hui-neng spoke the turning words which illuminated the situation and enlightened Ming. Hui-neng's response was so fitting and penetrating because it sprang directly from the Unconscious, where all is the synchronous play of one mind.

After parting from Ming, Hui-neng lived in hiding for fifteen years. He emerged by instructing two monks arguing over the flapping of a flag. One said that the flag was moving; the other that the wind was moving. Hui-neng told them, "It is your mind that is moving." His identity was determined, and for the next thirty-seven years Hui-neng taught that seeing into one's Self-nature in an instantaneous, transcendent intuition was the essence of Zen. He died quietly at the age of seventy-six after giving his disciples his last instructions.

According to Suzuki, Hui-neng revolutionized Zen with his teachings of ontological emptiness and *prajna*, transcendent intuition or wisdom, which he described as an instantaneous seeing into the Original Nature.

> When Hui-neng declared, "From the first not a thing is," the keynote of his Zen thought was struck, and from it we recognize the extent of the difference between him and his predecessors and contemporaries. This keynote was never so clearly struck before. When the masters who preceded him pointed to the presence of Mind in each individual mind and also to its absolute purity, this idea of presence and purity was understood somehow to suggest the existence of an individual body, however transparent and ethereal it may be conceived. The result was to make digging this body out from the heap of obscuring materials the end of practice. On the other hand, Hui-neng's concept of nothingness may push one down into a bottomless abyss, which will no doubt create a feeling of utter forlornness.[2]

> "Seeing into one's own Nature" is the most significant phrase ever coined in Zen Buddhism. Around this Zen crystallized, and. . . its progress was rapid. . . . By "Nature" he understood Buddha-nature, or more particularly from the intellectual view, prajna. . . Prajna fills the universe, and never rests from work. It is free, creative, and at the same time it knows itself. It knows all in one and one in all. This mysterious working of prajna issues from your own Nature.[3]

Fragments of Hui-neng's sermons were compiled in a volume entitled *The Platform Sutra*. Aside from the teachings ascribed to the Buddha and those who knew him, only this volume is honored as a sutra in Zen. Excerpts follow.

THE PLATFORM SUTRA

In my teaching what is most fundamental is Meditation and Wisdom. Do not be deceived and led to thinking that they are separable. They are one, and not two. Meditation is the Body of Wisdom, and Wisdom is the Use of Meditation. When Wisdom is taken up, Meditation is in Wisdom; when Meditation is taken up, Wisdom is in it.[4]

Meditation is not to get attached to the mind, is not to get attached to purity, nor is it to concern itself with immovability. It is not to be obstructed in all things, not to have any thought stirred up by the outside conditions of life, good and bad. Inwardly to see the immovability of one's Self-nature, outwardly to be free from the notion of form—this is Meditation.[5]

In Original Nature itself is intutive wisdom, and because of this, self-knowledge. Nature reflects itself in itself which is self-illumination not to be expressed in words.[6]

As long as there is a dualistic way of looking at things, there is no emancipation. Light stands against darkness; the passions stand against enlightenment. Unless these opposites are illuminated by transcendental intuition, so that the gap between the two are bridged, there is no understanding of the Mahayana. When you stay at one end of the bridge and are not able to grasp the oneness of the Buddha-nature, you are not one of us. The Buddha-nature knows neither decrease nor increase, whether it is in the Buddha or in common mortals. When it is within the passions, it is not defiled; when it is meditated upon, it does not thereby become purer. It is neither annihilated nor abiding; it neither comes nor departs; it is neither in the middle nor at either end; it neither dies nor is born. It remains the same all the time, unchanged in all changes. As it is never born, it never dies. It is not that we replace death with life but that the Buddha-nature is above birth-and-death. The main point is not to think of things good and bad and thereby to be restricted, but to let the mind move on as it is in itself and perform its inexhaustible functions. This is the way to be in accord with the Mind essence.[7]

To have an insight for once is to know what Buddhahood means. When the light of prajna penetrates the ground nature of consciousness, it illuminates inside and outside; everything grows transparent; and one recognizes one's own inmost mind. To recognize the inmost mind is emancipation. When emancipation is attained, prajna-samadhi obtains. To realize prajna-samadhi means to have the Unconscious.

What is the Unconscious? It is to see all things as they are and not to become attached to anything; it is to be present in all places and yet not to become attached anywhere; it is to remain forever in the purity of Self-nature; it is to let the six sense-robbers run out of the six sense-gates into the world of the six sense-objects, and yet not to become defiled therein, nor to get away therefrom; it is but to retain perfect freedom in going and coming. This is to realize prajna-samadhi, to be master of one-self, to become emancipated, and is known as living the Unconscious. But if no thought arises on anything whatever, this means the cessation of consciousness. Such are in the bondage of the Dharma; it is a one-sided view.[8]

All the Buddhas of the past, present, and future, and all the sutras. . . are in the Self-nature of each individual where they were from the first. . . . There is within oneself that which knows, and thereby one has an enlightenment.[9]

Lin-chi I-hsuan

Between Hui-neng and Lin-chi came four illustrious masters in the Golden Age of Zen in China: Nan-yueh, Ma-tsu, Po-chang, and Huang-po. When Hui-neng met Nan-yueh, he asked him, "Where do you come from?" Nan-yueh replied, "I come from Tung-shan." "What is it that so comes?" asked Hui-neng. It took Nan-yueh six years before he could answer, "Even when it is said to be something, the mark is already missed!"[1]

When Nan-yueh met Ma-tsu, the latter was doing nothing but zazen day and night. One day Nan-yueh asked him, "What are you trying to accomplish, Reverend Sir?" Ma-tsu said, "I am trying to become a Buddha." Nan-yueh walked away without a word, picked up a piece of brick, and started to polish it. Ma-tsu asked, "What are you doing?" Nan-yueh said, "I am making a mirror." Ma-tsu further asked, "Can polishing a brick make it into a mirror?" Nan-yueh retorted, "Can doing zazen make one into a Buddha?" Ma-tsu asked, "What should I do then?" Nan-yueh replied, "It is like putting a cart to an ox. When the cart does not move, which is better, to beat the cart or the ox?" Ma-tsu was unable to answer. Nan-yueh then explained, "If you want to learn to do zazen, know that Zen is not in sitting or lying. If you want to become a Buddha by sitting, know that the Buddha has no fixed form. Never discriminate in living the Dharma

31

of nonattachment. If you try to become a Buddha by sitting, you are killing Buddha. If you attach to the form of sitting, you can never attain Buddhahood."[2]

Ma-tsu gave two famous answers to the question, "What is Buddha?" First he said, "Mind is Buddha," and later, "No mind, no Buddha." On another occasion when he was asked, "What kind of man does not keep company with anything?", he replied, "I will tell you when you swallow the water of the West River in one gulp."[3] One day after a flock of wild geese flew by, Ma-tsu asked Po-chang, "What are they?" "They are wild geese," said Po-chang. "Where are they flying?" asked Ma-tsu. "They are already gone," answered Po-chang. Ma-tsu then suddenly grabbed Po-chang's nose and wrenched it. Po-chang cried in pain. "You say they have flown away, but all the same they have been here from the beginning," said Ma-tsu. Po-chang broke into a cold sweat and was enlightened. The next day Ma-tsu was about to give a talk when Po-chang came forward and rolled up the mat to end the talk. Without protesting Ma-tsu came down from his seat and returned to his room. He then called Po-chang and asked why he had rolled up the mat. Po-chang said, "Yesterday you twisted my nose, and it was quite painful." Ma-tsu asked, "Where was your thought wandering then?" "It is not painful anymore, Master," replied Po-chang.[4] Years later Po-chang once again came to Ma-tsu for instruction. Ma-tsu gave a loud shout "Katsu!" which crushed everything in him and deafened him for three days.

Po-chang established work as an integral part of the monastic order. Out of concern for his health the monks hid his farming tools, since Po-chang refused to rest even in his old age. When he could not find them, he retired to his room but then refused to eat, saying, "A day without work, a day without eating."[5] One day a visitor came seeking an abbot for a monastery. Po-chang called his monks. The visitor asked them to walk three steps and clear their throats to determine their worthiness. Beginning with the head monk, none of the monks could pass this test except the cook monk, who was immediately approved. The head monk protested the evaluation, however, so Ma-tsu gave his own test. He placed a pitcher on the floor and said, "Do not call this a pitcher. What do you call it? The head monk said, "It cannot be called a piece of wood." The cook monk simply kicked the pitcher over with his foot. Ma-tsu proclaimed, "Head monk you have been outdone by this cook monk." Eventually Po-chang transmitted the Dharma to Huang-po, saying, "When the disciple's insight is identical with that of the master, the master's power is diminished by half. When the disciple's insight surpasses that of the master, then he is worthy of receiving the transmission."[7]

There is a famous story about Huang-po pointing out the true Self to a governor. Visiting a temple, the governor pointed to a portrait and asked the abbot, "Who is he?" The abbot answered, "The late abbot." The governor then asked, "Here is his portrait, and where is the person?" The abbot could not answer, but the governor was insistent. Unable to find anyone who could, the abbot finally thought of a monk who had come for lodging and spent his time cleaning the courtyards. Huang-po was called, and the governor asked him, "Venerable Sir, these gentlemen are unfortunately unwilling to answer my question. Will you be good enough to undertake the task?" "What is the question?" Huang-po said. The governor repeated the question, "Here is the portrait of the former abbot, and where is the person?" At once Huang-po called out, "Governor!" "Yes!" responded the governor. "Where is he?" answered Huang-po.[8]

Lin-chi I-hsuan was born between 810 and 815 and was already a well-versed Buddhist scholar when he decided to study Zen under Huang-po in his twenties. Plain and direct in his behavior, Lin-chi trained for three years without asking a single question. The head monk recognized his potential and urged him to approach the master. He told Lin-chi just to ask what the cardinal principle of Buddhism was. Lin-chi went, but before he had finished speaking, Huang-po hit him. Lin-chi did not understand, but the head monk urged him to try again. The same thing happened again and again. Lin-chi regretted the karma preventing him from understanding and decided to leave. Meanwhile the head monk praised Lin-chi to Huang-po, so when Lin-chi came to take his leave, Huang-po advised him to see Ta-yu.

Meeting Ta-yu, Lin-chi said, "Three times I asked Huang-po what the cardinal principle of Buddhism was and three times he hit me. I don't know whether I was at fault or not."

> "Huang-po is such a grandmother that he utterly exhausted himself with your troubles!" said Ta-yu. "And now you come here asking whether you were at fault or not!"
> At these words Lin-chi attained great enlightenment. "Ah, there isn't so much to Huang-po's Buddha-dharma!" he cried.
> Ta-yu grabbed Lin-chi and said, "You bed-wetting little devil! You just finished asking whether you were at fault or not, and

now you say, 'There isn't so much to Huang-po's Buddha-dharma.' What did you see? Speak, speak!"

Lin-chi jabbed Ta-yu in the side three times. Shoving him away, Ta-yu said, "You have Huang-po for a teacher. It's not my business."

Lin-chi left Ta-yu and returned to Huang-po. Huang-po saw him coming and said, "What a fellow! Coming and going, coming and going—when will it end!"

"It's all due to your grandmotherly kindness," Lin-chi said, and then presented the customary gift and stood waiting.

"Where have you been?" asked Huang-po.

"Recently you deigned to favor me by sending me to see Ta-yu," said Lin-chi.

"What did Ta-yu have to say?" asked Huang-po.

Lin-chi then related what happened. Huang-po said, "How I'd like to catch that fellow and give him a good dose of the stick!"

"Why say you'd 'like to'? Take it right now!" said Lin-chi and immediately gave Huang-po a slap.

"You lunatic!" cried Huang-po. "Coming back here and pulling the tiger's whiskers."

Lin-chi gave a shout.

"Attendant, get this lunatic out of here and take him to the Monk's Hall," said Huang-po.[9]

Lin-chi trained with Huang-po for ten more years. Their interaction set the rigorous, martial, and free spirit of this line of Zen. Once Lin-chi was hoeing. When he saw Huang-po coming, he stopped and leaned on his hoe. "Is this guy tired already?" said Huang-po. "I haven't lifted my hoe yet. How could I be tired?" answered Lin-chi. Huang-po hit him. Lin-chi grabbed Huang-po's stick, jabbed him with it, and knocked him down. Huang-po called a senior monk to help him up. Running over the senior monk said, "Huang-po, how can you let this lunatic get away with such rudeness!" Huang-po no sooner got to his feet than he hit the monk. Hoeing the ground, Lin-chi said, "Everywhere else the dead are cremated, but here I bury them alive at once."[10]

Once when Huang-po saw Lin-chi sleeping in the Monk's Hall, he struck the front plank of the sitting platform. Lin-chi lifted his head, saw it was Huang-po, and went back to sleep. Huang-po struck the front plank again and went to the upper part of the hall. Seeing the head monk sitting in meditation, he said, "That youngster down there is sitting in meditation. What are you doing cooking up wild fancies here!" "What's this old man up to?" said the head monk. Huang-po struck the front plank once more and left.[11]

On another occasion Lin-chi was lagging back as the monks went to the fields. Huang-po turned and seeing Lin-chi was empty-handed, asked, "Where is your hoe?" "Somebody took it from me," said Lin-chi. "Come here," said Huang-po, "I want to talk the matter over with you." Lin-chi stepped forward. Huang-po held his hoe up and said, "Just *this* people on the earth cannot hold up." Lin-chi snatched it from Huang-po's grasp and held it high. "Then why is it in my hands now?" he asked. "Today there's a man who's really working," said Huang-po returning to the temple.[12]

One day Lin-chi took his leave of Huang-po. Huang-po asked, "Where are you going?" Lin-chi replied, "If I don't go to Ho-nan, I'll return to Ho-pei." Huang-po hit him. Lin-chi seized Huang-po and gave him a slap. Laughing heartily, Huang-po called to his attendant, "Bring me the back rest and arm rest that belonged to my late teacher Po-chang." "Attendant, bring me some fire!" cried Lin-chi. Huang-po said, "Be that as it may, just take them with you. In the future you'll sit upon the tongue of every man on earth."[13]

After leaving Huang-po, Lin-chi went on a long pilgrimage visiting other masters along the way. He settled in a small temple around 850 and taught there about ten years and then retired. In 866, when he was about to die, he seated himself and said, "After I am extinguished, do not let my True Dharma Eye be extinguished." A monk came forward and said, "How could I let your True Dharma Eye be extinguished!" Lin-chi asked, "When somebody asks you about it, what will you say to him?" The monk gave a shout. "Who would have thought my True Dharma Eye would be extinguished upon reaching this blind ass!" said Lin-chi. Then sitting erect, he died.[14]

The central principle of Lin-chi's teachings was the True Man without Title who makes himself the master of every situation. He emphasized the working aspect of enlightenment and demanded that insight be manifest immediately in behavior. Omori Roshi elaborates:

> The center of development of Lin-chi's thinking is this "Man" — it pivots on that one word. Lin-chi certainly does not mean a Buddha nature which is only a potential, nor a body nature which exists within; but his special standpoint is that this five-foot bag of shit itself is to be grasped as the True Man without Title.
>
> Mu-I (without title) is sometimes expressed as Mu-E (without clothing) meaning transcendence of all dependence — absolutely naked without a stitch on. Since the Mu-I is the Mu-E, that man

limited by his five-foot-tall body and his fifty years of life *is* the absolutely existent without any dependence. The True Man without Title, casting away the red lump of flesh itself stands clear; the man of the way is an individual and at the same time transcends individuality—transcendent and at the same time individual.

In our physical body there is absolutely free human nature unlimited by anything at all. From morning to night, with the eye seeing things, with the ear hearing things, with the nose smelling odors, with the body feeling warm and cold, with the intellect appreciating things, with the hands grasping, with the feet walking—it is ever at work. Those who have not clearly realized this in experience, now, here, see and grasp it![15]

Lin-chi's teachings and incidents from his life are contained in *The Record of Lin-chi*. Excerpts follow:

THE RECORD OF LIN-CHI

The governor and his officers invited the master to take the high seat. The master said, "If the mountain priest goes up today, it is because there is no alternative; it is out of respect for the people. The tradition of our line of patriarchs and pupils is to hold the tongue. But then you would have nowhere to put a foot. In face of the governor's insistence, how can the mountain priest this day hide the great transmission?

"Well, is there here any skillful general to plant his banner and deploy his troops on the field? Let him testify before everyone, and we will see!"

A monk asked, "What is the great meaning of Buddhism?"

The Master gave a Katsu! shout. The monk bowed. The Master said, "That's a man who can hold his own in debate."[16]

The Master said, "On the lump of red flesh there is a True Man without Title, always coming out and in from your face. You who have not realized him, look, look!" Then a monk came up and asked, "What is this True Man without Title?" The Master came down from the Zen chair and caught hold of him, "Speak, speak!" The monk was at a loss. The Master released him, saying "True Man without Title—oh, what is this dried shit-stick!" And he returned to his quarters.[17]

The Master addressed the assembly, saying, "Followers of the Way, as to Buddha-dharma no effort is necessary. You have only to be ordinary with nothing to do—defecating, urinating, putting on clothes, eating food, and lying down when tired.

Fools laugh at me, but
The wise man understands.

A man of old said:

To make work on the outside
Is just being a blockhead.

"Just make yourself master of every situation, and wherever you stand is the true place. No matter what circumstances come they cannot dislodge you [from where you stand.] Even though you bear the remaining influences of past delusions or the karma from [having committed] the five heinous crimes (patricide, matricide, killing a saint, shedding the blood of a Buddha, and disrupting the community of seekers), these of themselves become the ocean of emancipation."[18] (Brackets mine)

The Master addressed the assembly, saying, "Men who today study the Way must have faith in themselves. Don't seek outside! But you just go on clambering after the realm of worthless dust, never distinguishing the false from the true. . . . .

"Resolute men, don't just pass your days in discussion and idle talk, arguing about authorities and outlaws, right and wrong, licentiousness and wealth. As for me, whoever comes here, whether he be monk or layman, I discern him through and through. Regardless of the manner in which he presents himself, as far as [his] words and phrases are concerned, they are all dreams and illusions. On the other hand, it is obvious that the man who avails himself of every circumstance is [embodying] the mysterious principle of all the buddhas. The state of buddhahood does not itself proclaim, "I am the state of buddhahood!"; rather than that, this very man of the Way, who is dependent upon nothing, comes forth availing himself of every state.

"If someone comes forth and asks me about seeking Buddha, I immediately appear in conformity with the state of purity; if someone asks me about bodhisattvahood, I immediately appear in conformity with the state of compassion; if someone asks me about Bodhi (True Wisdom), I immediately appear in conformity with the state of pure mystery; if someone asks me about Nirvana, I immediately appear in conformity with the state of serene stillness. Though there be ten thousand differentiated states, the man himself does not differ. Therefore,

According with [the] things he manifests a form,
Like the moon [reflecting] on the water.

"Followers of the Way, if you want to accord with Dharma as is, just be men of great resolve. If you spinelessly shilly-shally along, you're good for nothing. Just as a cracked jug is unfit to hold ghee, so he who would be a great vessel [of Dharma] must not be taken in by the deluded views of others. Make yourself master everywhere, and wherever you stand is the true [place].

"Whatever comes along, don't accept any of it. One thought of doubt, and instantly the demon [Mara] enters your mind. When even a bodhisattva doubts, the demon of birth-and-death takes the advantage. Just desist from thinking, and never seek outside. If something should come, illumine it. Just have faith in your activity revealed now—there isn't a thing to do.

One thought of your mind produces the three realms and, in accordance with causal conditions and influenced by circumstances, the division into the six dusts (the five senses and objects of mind) takes place. What is lacking in your present responsive activity! In an instant you enter the pure, enter the dirty. . . and everywhere you travel all you see is empty names.[19] (Brackets mine)

Hakuin Ekaku

After Lin-chi came sixteen Chinese patriarchs before Nanpo Shomyo, better known as Kaio Kokushi, transmitted the Yogi line of Rinzai Zen to Japan in 1267. In all over twenty-four schools of Zen were transmitted from China to Japan eventually.

At his initiation as head abbot of an important temple, he said that his coming was from nowhere and that one year later his going would be to nowhere. He died exactly a year later.[1]

Nanpo was succeeded by Shuho Myocho, better known as Daito Kokushi. Following Nanpo's death, Shuho hid himself among beggars under a bridge for twenty years to refine himself by living under miserable conditions. Once a degraded samurai came to test a new sword on a beggar. Shuho told the others to hide and sat in meditation. The samurai approached, drew his sword, and shouted, "Get ready, my sword is going to cut you in half!" Shuho did not move. An awe came over the samurai who hesitated and then retreated.[2]

Emperor Hanazono found Shuho eventually by passing out a kind of melon Shuho loved to the beggars. When Hanazono saw the brilliance in Shuho's eyes, he said, "Take this melon without using your hands." "Give it to me without using your hands," Shuho responded.[3] Shuho thus became the teacher of the emperor.

On another occasion the emperor asked Shuho, "Who is he who remains companionless within the ten thousand things?" Shuho

moved his fan and said, "I have long enjoyed being bathed in the Imperial breeze."⁴ For many years Shuho had been unable to meditate in the full lotus position because of a crippled leg. When he felt death approaching, he broke his leg with his own hands and took the full lotus. Then, despite agonizing pain, he wrote his final words and died with the last stroke of the brush.

> *Buddhas and patriarchs cut to pieces;*
> *The sword is ever kept sharpened.*
> *Where the wheel turns,*
> *The void gnashes its teeth.*⁵

Shuho's successor, Kanzan Igen, became a monk in his youth but was fifty by the time he met Shuho. After two years of struggle, Kanzan had his final realization. For the next eight years, Kanzan worked as a hired laborer tending cattle or tilling fields during the day, and at night sat zazen on a narrow shelf jutting out from the face of a high cliff. He started teaching at sixty, never lectured, and accepted only a few students whom he trained with extreme severity. Kanzan died standing quietly beside a temple pond.⁶

The line of these three patriarchs came to be known as the O-To-Kan School by taking O from Kaio Kokushi, To from Daito Kokushi, and Kan from Kanzan Igen. It flourished in the thirteenth century under the patronage of the samurai who found in it a viable way to transcend death since it relied on willpower rather than learning. Eventually a style of Zen called Nio Zen emerged. Shozan (1579-1655), a distinguished samurai before taking the Buddhist vows, said:

> In studying Zen you should take Buddhist images for models, but that of the Tathagata (the manifested Buddha) does not suit the beginner because the Tathagata type of zazen is beyond him. Rather model yourself on images of Nio and Fudo (the Diamond Deity and the Deity of Immovable Wisdom, two indomitable guardians of ferocious mien) both of which are symbolic of discipline.
>
> Unfortunately, Buddhism has declined from bad to worse with the result that most are milksops critically lacking in vigor. Only the valorous can train properly. The ignorant being mild and sanctimonious are mistaken in the belief that such is the way of Buddhist practice. Then there are the madmen bagatelle. Myself, I am a stranger to sanctimoniousness and satorishness, my sole aim being to conquer all with a vivacious mind. Sharing

the vitality of Nio and Fudo, exterminate all your evil karma and passions. (Here the Master paused, eyes set, hands clenched, teeth gnashing.) Guard yourself closely, and nothing will be able to interfere. Only bravery will carry you through. We'll have no part of weaklings here! Be wide awake, and attain the vigor living Zen.

You had better practice zazen while busily occupied. The samurai's zazen must be the sort that will support him in the midst of battle, when he is threatened by guns and spears. After all, what use can the tranquilizing type of sitting be on the battlefield? You should foster the Nio spirit above all. All worldly arts are cultivated through Zen-sitting. The military arts especially cannot be practiced with a feeble spirit. (So saying, the Master pretended to draw a sword.) Zazen must be virile, yet the warrior upholds it only in battle; no sooner does he sheathe his sword than he's off guard again. The Buddhist, on the other hand, always maintains his vigor. Never is he a loser. The more he ripens in discipline, the more adept he becomes in everything, from the recitation of a text to tapping a hand drum in Noh. Perfect in all virtues, he can fit in anywhere.[7]

Fourteen patriarchs after Kanzan came Dokyo Etan. Once when his village was beset by wolves, Dokyo sat for seven nights in different graveyards to test his samadhi while wolves sniffed at his throat.[8] At the age of eighty Dokyo wrote his parting verse and died laughing.

In the frantic hurry of dying
It's difficult to utter the last words.
If I were to speak a wordless word,
I wouldn't speak, I wouldn't speak.[9]

By the seventeenth century, Zen was well established in Japanese society but was in danger of degenerating into a cultural pastime practiced by monks devoted to aesthetics rather than spiritual training. It was Hakuin Ekaku, Dokyo's successor, who restored enlightenment based on rigorous training as the essence of Zen, and thus is honored as The Patriarch who Revived Zen. He was born as the youngest of five children in 1686 to a commoner family.[10] As a child he was bold, quick, strong, and highly sensitive to the impermanence of life. He had a remarkable memory and at four knew over three hundred local songs by heart. At eight he heard a sutra chanted at a religious service and recited it verbatim upon returning home.

At eleven he was terrified by a priest's vivid description of the

Buddhist hells and began to worry about how precariously life
seemed poised over eternal torment. In secret he took to chanting
sutras day and night for his salvation. One day when he was bathing
with his mother, she asked that the fire be made hotter. As more
firewood was added, his skin began to prickle with the heat and the
iron bath cauldron began to rumble. He let out a scream of terror
which resounded throughout the neighborhood. From this time he
resolved to become a monk, and despite his parents' protests, at fifteen he entered Shoin-ji, a small temple in his village.

Hoping to find profound and mysterious doctrines, Hakuin studied the Lotus Sutra extensively, but after a year concluded that it
was just another book. His despair deepened when at nineteen he
read about the death of Master Ganto. Ganto remained in his temple after the others had fled from bandits. One of them speared him,
and though Ganto's expression did not change, he gave a cry that
was heard for miles as he died. Hakuin felt that if even such a great
master could not save himself from a bandit, he had no chance at all
to save himself from hell. Losing his faith in Buddhism, he considered abandoning spiritual discipline and amusing himself with poetry
and fiction. He drifted from temple to temple until one day he decided to settle the direction of his life by randomly picking a book from
a collection being aired. He opened it and happened on the story of
a Chinese master who sat in meditation throughout the night and
drove a gimlet into his thigh to keep awake. He found new inspiration in this story and committed himself to Zen.

Hakuin traveled to various temples and trained intensely for the
next four years and had two realizations. But he was disappointed in
being unable to attain a pure state of undistracted meditation where
waking and sleeping were the same. At twenty-four, however, he felt
sure he had had an enlightenment unsurpassed in several hundred
years.

Night and day I did not sleep; I forgot both to eat and rest.
Suddenly a great doubt manifested itself before me. It was as
though I was frozen solid in the midst of an ice sheet extending
tens of thousands of miles. A purity filled my breast and I could
neither go forward nor retreat. To all intents and purposes I was
out of my mind and the Mu alone remained. Although I sat in
the lecture hall and listened to the Master's lecture, it was as
though I were hearing a discussion from a distance outside the
hall. At times it felt as though I were floating through the air.

This state lasted for several days. Then I chanced to hear the
sound of the temple bell and I was suddenly transformed. It was

as if a sheet of ice had been smashed or a jade tower had fallen with a crash. Suddenly I returned to my senses. I felt then that I had achieved the status of Yen-t'ou (Ganto) who through the three periods of time encountered not the slightest loss (although he had been murdered by bandits). All my former doubts vanished as though ice had melted away. In a loud voice I called, "Wonderful, wonderful! There is no cycle of birth and death through which one must pass. There is no enlightenment one must seek. The seventeen hundred koans handed down from the past have not the slightest value whatsoever. My pride soared up like a majestic mountain, my arrogance surged forward like the tide. Smugly I thought to myself, 'In the past two or three hundred years no one could have accomplished such a marvelous breakthrough as this.' "[11] (Parentheses mine)

Hakuin presented his realization to the master of the temple and fellow disciples. They did not approve fully, but Hakuin still burned with conviction and was advised to see Dokyo Etan, better known as Shoju.

Upon meeting Master Shoju, Hakuin presented a verse. But Shoju dismissed this as academic and demanded an intuitive expression. Hakuin replied, "If there were something intuitive that I could show you, I'd vomit it out," and made a gagging sound. Shoju then said, "Tell me, what is Joshu's Mu?" Hakuin elatedly replied, "Pervading the universe. Nowhere to take hold of it!" Shoju grabbed Hakuin's nose, twisted it, laughed heartily, and said, "I am quite at ease to take hold of it." He then released it and ridiculed Hakuin, "You dead monk in a cave! Are you satisfied with such a Mu?" Shoju smashed Hakuin's self-satisfaction and whenever he saw him, called him a dead monk in a cave.

One evening while Shoju was cooling himself on a veranda, Hakuin presented a verse. "Delusions and fancies," Shoju said. Hakuin shouted back, "Delusions and fancies!" Shoju then seized him, rained twenty or thirty blows on him, and pushed him off the veranda. Hakuin lay in the mud scarcely breathing and barely conscious. Shoju roared with laughter from above. Recovering after a short while, Hakuin got up and perspiring profusely, bowed to Shoju. Shoju said, "You dead monk in a cave!" After further intense training, Hakuin presented still another understanding, but Shoju just said, "You dead monk in a cave."

After eight months of such harsh treatment, Hakuin began to think of leaving. But one day while begging before an old lady's house, he slipped into a deep meditation. He became oblivious to all, and the old lady kept repeating that she had nothing to give him. Angered by his seeming obstinacy, the old lady struck him on the head with a broom. Coming to his senses, Hakuin found that formerly impenetrable koans were clear to him. When he expressed his new understanding to Shoju, Shoju said nothing but only laughed pleasantly and ceased calling Hakuin a dead monk in a cave. Hakuin also dreamt that his mother told him that his spiritual merits had gained her a Buddhist paradise. Soon after Hakuin left to attend a former teacher who had fallen ill. Shoju warned him to continue training and not to hope for more than one or two good disciples.

Hakuin redoubled his efforts only to suffer a psychophysical breakdown:

> Teeth clenched and eyes aglare, I sought to free myself from food and sleep. Before a month had passed the heart fire mounted to my head; my lungs were burning, but my legs felt as if freezing in ice and snow. In my ears was a rushing sound as of a stream in a valley. My courage failed, and I felt constant fear. I felt spiritually exhausted, night and day seeing dreams, my armpits always wet with sweat, and my eyes full of tears.[12]

Eventually his search for a cure led him to Hakuyu, a Taoist sage living in a remote, ethereal mountain setting. Finally moved by Hakuin's persistent pleas, Hakuyu instructed him in *naikan* (literally, inner looking), a method of circulating the vital energy of the body based on Taoist alchemy. Excerpts from these instructions follow:

> From the mounting of the heart-fire your grievous illness has arisen. . . .Now it may be that as my outward appearance is Taoist, you fancy that my teaching is far from Buddhism. But this is Zen. One day when you break through, you will see how laughable were your former ideas.[13]

> It is essential to keep the upper parts of the body cool and the lower parts warm. You must know that to nourish the body it is imperative that the vital energy be made to fill its lower part. Frequently people say that the divine elixir is the distillation of the five elements, but they are unaware that the five elements, water, fire, wood, metal, and earth, are associated with the five sense organs: the eyes, ears, nose, tongue, and body. How does one bring together these five organs in order to distill the divine

elixir? For this we have the law of the five non-outflowings:
when the eye does not see recklessly, when the ear does not hear
recklessly, when the tongue does not taste recklessly, when the
body does not feel recklessly, when the consciousness does not
think recklessly, then the turgid primal energy accumulates
before your very eyes. This is the "vast physical energy" of
which Mencius speaks. If you draw this energy and concentrate
it in the space below the navel; if you distill it over the years,
protect it to the utmost, and nourish it constantly, then before
you know it the elixir-oven and the whole universe becomes a
mass of this great circulating elixir. Then you will awaken to
the fact that you yourself are a divine sage with true immortal-
ity, one who was not born before heaven and earth were formed
and who will not die after empty space has vanished.[14]

If the student finds in his meditation that the four great ele-
ments are out of harmony, and mind and body are fatigued, he
should rouse himself and make this meditation. Let him visual-
ize on the crown of his head that celestial So ointment about as
much as a duck's egg, pure in color and fragrance. (Hakuin's
recipe calls for such things as one part of the "real aspect of
things," two parts of "without desires," a dash of "intuitive
wisdom," and so on. It is perhaps enough to imagine the ointment as vital energy.) Let him feel its exquisite essence and
flavor melting and filtering down through his head, its flow per-
meating downwards, slowly laving the shoulders and elbows, the
sides of the breast and within the chest, the lungs, liver, stomach,
and internal organs and six auxilliaries follow the mind downwards. There is a sound like trickling water. Percolating through
the whole body, the flow goes gently down the legs, stopping at
the soles of the feet. . . .Just as a skillful physician collects herbs
of rare fragrance and puts them in a pan to boil, so the student
feels that from the navel down he is simmering in the So elixir.
When this meditation is being done, there will be psychological
experiences of a sudden indescribable fragrance at the nose-tip,
of a gentle and exquisite sensation in the body. Mind and body
become harmonized and far surpass their condition at the peak
of youth. . . The organs are tranquilized, and insensibly the skin
begins to glow. If the practice is carried on without relapse, what
illness will not be healed, what power will not be acquired, what
perfection will not be attained, what Way will not be fulfilled.[15]

Hakuin cured himself with naikan and meditated in isolation for several years under conditions of great austerity. He experienced six or seven great realizations and countless minor ones, and eventually attained a tremendous vitality. Studying the sutras, he quoted the phrase, "the ancient teachings illumine the heart, and the heart illumines the ancient teachings," to describe his own experience. Several times he heard a music in the sky which stopped when he recognized it as his own mind. Once he was overwhelmed by fear which he finally dissipated by the meditation, "By what is this fear experienced?"[16]

At the age of thirty-two Hakuin settled at the dilapidated temple of Shoin-ji with just one disciple. At the age of forty-one during a private meditation retreat, he had another dream about his mother in which she gave him a magnificent, purple, silk robe. He found two mirrors in the sleeves.

> The reflection from the mirror in the right sleeve penetrated to my heart and vital organs. My own mind, mountains and rivers, the great earth seemed serene and bottomless. The mirror in the left sleeve, however, gave off no reflection whatsoever. Its surface was like that of a new pan that had yet to be touched by flames. But it suddenly blazed with light, a million times brighter than the other. After this looking at the things of the world was like seeing my own face, and for the first time I understood how the Buddha sees the Buddha-nature within his eye.[17]

The next year while reading the Lotus Sutra at night, the chirping of a cricket suddenly awoke him to the depths of the sutra and the meaning of Shoju's daily life. This time no extreme reaction occurred in his mind and body, and he saw that he had been mistaken about his previous great realizations.

Hakuin taught at Shoin-ji for the next forty-one years. He was particularly concerned about the plight of the common people and spread Zen among them with paintings, songs, and simple sermons. In turn they held him in great esteem and affection. A famous story illustrates his unassailability and his compassion.

> A girl among the congregation became pregnant. Her severe father bullied her for the name of her lover, and in the end, thinking that if she said so she might escape punishment, she told him, "It is Zen Master Hakuin." The father said no more, but when the child was born he at once took it to him and threw the baby down, piling on every insult and sneer at the disgrace

of the affair. Hakuin only said, "Oh, is that so?" and took the
baby into his arms. Thereafter even during rainy days and stormy
nights, he would go out to beg milk from the neighboring houses.
Wherever he went he took the baby, wrapped in the sleeve of
his ragged robe. Now he who had been regarded as a living
Buddha, worshipped as a Shakamuni, had fallen indeed. Many
of the disciples who had flocked to him, turned against him, and
left. Hakuin still said not a word. Meantime the mother found
she could not bear the agony of separation from her child, and
further began to be afraid of the consequences in the next life of
what she had done. She confessed the name of the real father of
the child. Her own father, rigid in his conception of virtue,
became almost mad with fear. He rushed to Hakuin and prostrated himself, begging over and over for forgiveness. Hakuin
this time too said only, "Oh, is that so?" and gave him the child.[18]

In his old age Hakuin continued to be extraordinarily energetic.
He recorded:

> Even though I am past seventy now my vitality is ten times
> as great as it was when I was thirty or forty. My mind and body
> are strong, and I never feel that I absolutely must lie down to
> rest. Should I want to I find no difficulty in refraining from sleep
> for two, three, or even seven days, without suffering any decline
> in my mental powers. I am surrounded by three-to-five hundred
> demanding students, and even though I lecture on the scrip-
> tures or on the collections of the Masters' sayings for thirty to
> fifty days in a row, it does not exhaust me. I am quite convinced
> that all this is owing to the power gained from practicing this
> method of introspection (naikan).[19] (Parenthesis mine)

Hakuin died in his sleep at eighty-three. His artistic and literary
creations were profuse, but most impressively in a tradition where
developing even one disciple capable of transmitting the Dharma is
an acknowledged accomplishment, Hakuin left ninety such disciples.
He is thus honored as the greatest sage in five hundred years. He
called naikan and zazen the wings of his teachings, and the koan
"What is the sound of one hand clapping?" was his spiritual sword.

Regarding zazen, Hakuin disdained tranquil meditation and advo-
cated uninterrupted meditation which illuminated whatever circumstances one might encounter.

> For the mind that is master of true meditation, the space

below the navel is firm as though a huge rock were settled there, and when this mind functions in its awesome dignity, not one deluded thought may enter, not one discriminating idea can exist.[20]

Attain a state of mind in which, even though surrounded by crowds of people, it is as if you were alone in a field extending tens of thousands of miles.[21]

How does one obtain true enlightenment? In the busy round of mundane affairs, in the confusion of worldly problems, amidst the seven upside-downs and the eight upsets, behave as a valiant man would when surrounded by a host of enemies. Be a man who always attaches to himself the unsurpassed luster of the true, uninterrupted meditation, one who has no further need to demonstrate his activity, but has attained a state of mind that has extinguished both body and mind and has made all into an empty cave. At such a time, if one allows no fears to arise, and marches forward single-mindedly, one will suddenly be endowed with a great power. At all times in your study of Zen, fight against delusions and worldly thoughts, battle the black demon of sleep, attack concepts of the active and the passive, order and disorder, right and wrong, hate and love, and join battle with all things of the mundane world. Then in pushing forward with true meditation and struggling fiercely, there unexpectedly will be true enlightenment.[22]

In my later years I have come to the conclusion that the advantage in accomplishing true meditation lies distinctly in the favor of the warrior class. A warrior must from the beginning to the end be physically strong. In his attendance on his duties and in his relationships with others the most rigid punctiliousness and propriety are required. His hair must be properly dressed, his garments in the strictest of order, and his swords must be fastened at his side. With this exact and proper deportment, the true meditation stands forth with overflowing splendor. Mounted on a sturdy horse, the warrior can ride forth to face an uncountable horde of enemies as though he were riding into a place empty of people. The valiant, undaunted expression on his face reflects his practice of the peerless, true, uninterrupted meditation sitting. Meditating in this way, the warrior can accomplish in one month what it takes the monk a year to do; in three days he can open up for himself benefits that would take the monk a hundred days.[23]

Though his instructions below refer to the Mu koan, in his later
years Hakuin used the Sound of One Hand koan almost exclusively.
He taught that if one proceeded with great faith and great will in
the face of the great doubt raised by the koan, then realization was
assured.

> When a person faces the great doubt, before him there is in
> all directions only a vast and empty land without birth and with-
> out death, like a huge plain of ice extending ten thousand miles.
> . . .Without his senses he sits and forgets to stand, stands and
> forgets to sit. Within his heart there is not the slightest thought
> or emotion, only the single word Mu. It is as though he were
> standing in complete emptiness. At this time no fears arise, no
> thoughts creep in, and when he advances single-mindedly with-
> out retrogression, suddenly it will be as though a sheet of ice
> were broken or a jade tower had fallen. He will experience a
> great joy, one that never in forty years has he seen or heard. At
> this time "birth, death, and Nirvana will be like yesterday's
> dreams. . . ." This is known as the time of the great penetration
> of wondrous awakening, the state where the "Katsu!" is shouted.
> It cannot be handed down, it cannot be explained; it is just like
> knowing for yourself by drinking it whether water is hot or cold.
> The ten directions melt before the eyes, the three periods are
> penetrated in an instant of thought. What joy is there in the
> realms of man and Heaven that can compare with this?
> This power can be obtained in the space of three to five days
> if the student will advance determinedly. You may ask how one
> can make this great doubt appear. Do not favor a quiet place, do
> not shun a busy place, but always set in the tanden Chao-Chou's
> (Joshu's) Mu. Then, asking what principle this Mu contains, if
> you discard all emotions, concepts, and thoughts and investigate
> single-mindedly, there is no one before whom the great doubt
> will not appear. When you call forth this great doubt before you
> in its pure and uninvolved form, you may undergo an unpleas-
> ant and strange reaction. However, you must accept the fact that
> the realization of so felicitous a thing as the Great Matter, the
> trampling of the multi-tiered gate of birth and death that has
> come down through endless kalpas, the penetration of the inner
> understanding of the basic enlightenment of all the Tathagatas
> (another name for Buddha) of the ten directions, must involve a
> certain amount of suffering.[24] (Parentheses mine)

Hakuin's most famous writing is "The Song of Zazen" which is chanted daily in all Japanese Rinzai temples.

THE SONG OF ZAZEN

All beings are from the very beginning Buddhas.
It is like water and ice:
Apart from water, no ice,
Outside living beings, no Buddhas.
Not knowing it is near, they seek it afar. What a pity!
It is like one in water crying out from thirst;
It is like a rich man's son lost among the poor.
The cause of our circling through the six worlds
Is that we are on the dark paths of ignorance.
Dark path upon dark path treading,
When shall we escape from birth-and-death?
The Zen meditation of the Mahayana
Is beyond all our praise.
Giving and morality and the other perfections,
Chanting praises to the Buddha, repentance, discipline,
*   and the many other right actions,*
All come back to the practice of meditation.
The merit of even a single sitting
Erases countless sins of the past.
Where then are there wrong paths?
The Pure Land cannot be far away.
When in reverence this truth is heard even once,
He who praises it and faithfully follows it has merit
*   without end.*
But if you turn your eyes within
And confirm directly the truth of Self-nature,
That Self-nature is no nature.
You will have transcended vain words.
The gate opens, and cause and effect are one;
Straight ahead runs the way of non-duality,
*   non-trinity,*
Taking as form the form of no-form,
Going or returning, he is ever at home.
Taking as thought the thought of no-thought,

Singing and dancing, all is the voice of truth.
How boundless and free is the sky of Samadhi!
How refreshingly bring the moon of the fourfold
*   wisdom!*
What is there that you lack! Nirvana presents itself
*   before you!*
Where you stand is the Lotus Paradise;
Your person, the body of Buddha.[25]

Omori Sogen

Two generations after Hakuin the Rinzai school branched into the Takuju and Inzan lines. The Takuju line advances students through the koans faster and emphasizes the mysterious symbolism of words, while the Inzan line keeps the student on one koan until a penetrating realization is attained and stresses severe discipline.

One master of the Inzan line was Ryoen Genseki, five generations removed from Hakuin. In his youth Ryoen built a public bath and for three years rowed a boat to fetch mineral water, heated it, and invited neighboring peasants to use it. In his later years he never bathed in the water prepared for him by his disciple and washed instead with only two pailfuls. Nor did he eat more than one bowl of rice at a time, leaving the rest for poor children. After discovering he had cancer and being given a life expectancy of only several months, Ryoen dismissed the worries of his students and set off alone on a long pilgrimage. Ryoen lived for two more years. For nearly two weeks before his death, in critical condition, every morning he crawled from his room to the main hall of the temple where he invocated the names of the masters of his lineage. He needed to rest frequently throughout both his crawling and invocation. When he died, he was found sitting in the zazen position.[1] After Ryoen came Seisetsu Genjyo and Omori Sogen.

Besides the Zen tradition Omori was also deeply influenced by the tradition of *Bushido*, the Way of the samurai. Emerging during

the provincial wars which wracked Japan in the sixteenth century, the essence of Bushido consisted of the ability to face death unflinchingly in the service of the lord and clan. The *Hagakure*, a classic on Bushido, states:

> The Way of the Samurai is found in death. When it comes to either/or, there is only the quick choice of death. It is not particularly difficult. Be determined and advance. To say that dying without reaching one's aim is to die a dog's death is the frivolous way of sophisticates. When pressed with the choice of life or death, it is not necessary to gain one's aim.
>
> We all want to live. And in large part we make our logic according to what we like. But not having attained our aim and continuing to live is cowardice. This is a thin and dangerous line. To die without gaining one's aim *is* a dog's death and fanaticism. But there is no shame in this. This is the substance of the Way of the Samurai. If by setting one's heart right every morning and evening, one is able to live as though his body were already dead, he gains freedom in the Way. His whole life will be without blame, and he will succeed in his calling.[2]

To free themselves from the instinctual attachment to life, the samurai turned to Zen as a religion of will rather than learning. Zen training led them to die the Great Death and to awaken to their primal identity beyond life and death. Omori explains:

> The meaning here is to pass through or transcend death and killing to awaken to the "Great Life." This is the most serious matter of human existence. The people of old designated this experience as *Budo* (the martial Way). . . .The significance of this experience in the history of Japanese culture must never be undervalued. These individual experiences have occurred over and over, and it is this accumulation of experience that later developed *Budo* in Japan as a "Way for Man."[3]

Exemplifying the tradition of Bushido was Yamaoka Tesshu, one of the samurai instrumental in effecting the Meiji Restoration. Tesshu mastered Zen, *Kendo* (fencing), and *Shodo* (calligraphy). He was a giant of a man with enormous vitality. In his younger days he sat zazen so intensely that the rats in his house ran away. His wife reported that for ten years after their marriage he slept sitting up with one shoulder propped up by a bamboo sword. He could drink as much as four gallons of sake at one time.

In his mid-forties Yamaoka realized the ultimate meaning of the passage "When two swordpoints are crossed, there is no need to ward off. The best move is to return like the lotus flower blooming in the fire. Then just as you are, the energy of heaven-soaring spirits comes out of your original nature." At this time he also transcended the duality of man and woman. To a student intending to repress attachments, Yamaoka advised, "If you really mean to get rid of your passions, take courage now. Go and jump into their rough waves and see through them."

At a party commemorating the beginning of Yamaoka's fencing school, one student who had too much to drink threw up as he bowed in front of Yamaoka. Yamaoka stood up immediately, ate the vomit completely, and said in response to another student's disbelief, "I have just undergone discipline for the integration of purity and impurity."[4]

Once a visitor asked Yamaoka for a discourse on *The Record of Lin-chi.*

Yamaoka said, "Why sermons are given on it regularly at Engakuji. You'd better go and hear Master Kosen there."

The visitor replied, "I have been to hear him, but I still don't feel I really understand it. Now I know that you are an expert in fencing as well as Zen, and I have done quite a bit of fencing myself, so I thought perhaps it would be easier to understand it if I had an explanation from you."

"All right then, you had better change into fencing gear," and overruling the visitor's surprise, Yamaoka made him practice fencing till he was pouring with sweat and exhausted. After they had bathed and changed, they sat facing each other as before in the guest room.

Yamaoka asked, "Have you got it?"

"Got what?" asked the visitor. "I am here waiting to listen to you."

"That was the discourse you asked for. Zen masters in their temples teach it in their own way; that has nothing to do with me. I am a fencer and I teach it through fencing. You have had the explanation and that is all I have to give you."[5]

Yamaoka originated a method of Kendo training consisting of repeating contest after contest almost indefinitely, generally about one hundred in the morning and one hundred in the afternoon. Undergone only with special permission, the trial lasts from three to seven days. By the third day, though wrapped in soft silk inside protective gloves, the skin of the hands and fingers is apt to break and bleed. The disciple finds that he can no longer control his arms to hold the sword properly, that he can eat only semi-liquid food, and that he is so dehydrated his urine is red with blood. The first to undergo this training wrote:

> On the third day I could hardly raise myself from bed and had to ask my wife's help. When she tried to lift me, my body was cold like a lifeless corpse and she instinctively withdrew her hands. I felt her tears on my face. Hardening myself to the utmost, I admonished her not to be so weak-hearted. I had to use a cane to get to the training hall and be helped to put on my equipment.

> As soon as I took my position, the contestants began to crowd in. After a while one who was noted for thrusting his bamboo sword to the naked throat behind the protecting gorget and keeping it up even after he was struck over the head by his victorious opponent, asked the master for permission to participate. The master permitted him right away. When I saw him coming, I made up my mind this would be my last combat for I might not survive this contest. With this determination I felt the surging of new energy within myself. I was quite a different person. My sword returned to its proper position. I approached him and lifted the sword over my head to strike him with a blow. At that moment came the master's emphatic command to stop, and I dropped my sword.[6]

In his later years the fierceness of Yamaoka's discipline mellowed and instead of running away, the rats played all over him when he sat. At the age of fifty-three he died while sitting zazen. Today Omori Sogen is the successor to Yamaoka's line of calligraphy and lives in his old house.

Omori was born in 1904 and entered Zen through Kendo. He is a master of the Jikishinkage School of Kendo and did not become a monk until after Japan's defeat in World War II. Following the samurai tradition, Omori was about to commit seppuku with his comrades when his calligraphy teacher burst in and upbraided them for the selfishness of an act when more than ever Japan needed leadership. To Omori, his only recourse was to become a monk. After working on the koan Mu for eight years, Omori had a penetrating realization enabling him to pass through many other koans at once.

Omori made calligraphy and aspects of the *Hojo*, a sword form, into integral parts of Zen training. Below he describes a realization while practicing the Hojo, a sword form consisting of four parts patterned after the seasons.

The Hojo is to "remove all bad habits and addictions acquired since birth and to restore the original pure and bright permanent body." We might think of this body as one's Primal Face or Mu in Zen. What I am going to relate happened after I had practiced this technique for many years and was finally able to perform it freely. One day as I was practicing, my body was filled with energy. All muscular tension left my arms and legs, and I became conscious of the fact that the inward and outward forces in me had balanced each other out to zero. It was just as if I were weightless. . . .Later when I did zazen and entered samadhi, I noticed that I had achieved a balance of the mind, that my spiritual inward and outward forces had likewise balanced each other. This was a kind of realization. Afterwards it was very easy for me to reach this state, and I was able to sit very well.[7]

Omori has written extensively on Zen including commentaries on *The Record of Lin-chi* and the *The Blue Cliff Record*, as well as *Fencing and Zen*, and *An Introduction to Zen Discipline*. His books, however, have not been published in English yet. The following instructions have been excerpted from *An Introduction to Zen Discipline*.

AN INTRODUCTION TO ZEN DISCIPLINE

It is the aim of zazen to awaken us to our true selves by bringing us in touch with boundless life and the absoluteness of being. If once we touch the Absolute and return to our originally true selves, we are instantaneously liberated from the illusory perception caused by self-centered desires and delusions.

Since ancient times very few people have had an insight into the fact that Dharma is none other than zazen. This means that zazen is not the means of attaining any other purpose than zazen; and that zazen is not the way of learning Zen, but that zazen is something that makes us sit in zazen.

Master Sogaku writes, "If the kettle is put on and off the fire, the water will never come to a boil." Looking back over my past,

I am embarassed to confess that I was like that. Pupils who stop and resume their discipline alternately without being able to undergo discipline continuously must reflect over themselves. It is necessary for us to persevere and wish to sit everyday for at least one or two years. To do this we must entertain love for zazen and make steady efforts to deepen it. But we should remember that a certain degree of suffering is inevitable in spite of our love for zazen.

It goes without saying that we must choose as our masters those to whom the authentic teaching of Shakamuni has been transmitted through generations of Buddhist ancestors of India, China, and Japan in the same way as a bowl of water is poured intact into another bowl from generation to generation.

Master Seisetsu who was formerly my teacher entered the Tenryu-ji Monastery in 1893 at the age of seventeen. In the spring of the following year when he returned home, the first thing he did was visit his former teacher Priest Hokuin. He told Hokuin about the many things that had happened since he last saw him. Priest Hokuin, listening with great satisfaction and interest, suddenly asked, "By the way, what is the name of your teacher who was in charge of you in the monastery?" "Priest Gazan," said Seisetsu. "Gazan, it is an unfamiliar name. He must be a young priest. Whose religious heir is he?" Seisetsu replied, "I'm sorry I do not know." Hokuin looked sad and cried aloud, "What? You don't even know the religious lineage of your teacher? Ah, what kind of religious discipline have you undergone? I have never felt so miserable." Perhaps because of this incident it became a rule at Tenryu-ji to invocate the names of their Buddhist ancestors and hold a religious service for them the first thing each morning after Master Seisetsu came to preside there.

An authentic lineage is not enough, however, to make it possible for us to select the right teacher to discipline us through our lives. The master and disciple must really match with their *kiai* (vital energy) being one. However authentic the master, it will not be advantageous for the disciple to remain with him long if they are incompatible like fire and water in personality and temperament. Though beginners may not have an insight into the content of the transmission of their teacher, they will experience inspiration within themselves when they sincerely seek and meet a true master. One day when I was stressed to the point of breaking the stick used to hit monks, the sight of Master Seisetsu worshipping the image of the Buddha filled me with such exhilirating courage. In his talks, too, I felt such power emanating from his words. If we can perceive such awe-inspiring power in our teacher, we will be able to follow him without fail.

As we advance in meditation and the power of our concentration increases, there sometimes appear many phenomena during meditation, some disturbing and some pleasant. As a whole they have been called *makyo*, phenomena of the devil's realm, since old times. Some of the disturbing makyo are evidently harmful to our progress in Zen discipline, but it is easy to think of some way to drive them away. Pleasant makyo are a little harder to deal with. As if they had seen nothingness, some disciples often say in high spirits, "All the surroundings became purely white" or "My body rose directly to Heaven and spread all over." I said similar things in self-satisfaction to my teacher when he kidded me saying, "Perhaps you were asleep." But before we ourselves find them to be makyo, we presumptuously think that our teacher is ignorant of this state of samadhi. . . .When we come face to face with makyo, we should brace our minds and bodies, stir up our courage, and break them all to pieces, paying no attention to them.

Ordinarily when we sit in zazen, our dispersed minds become resolutely unified like immovable water profoundly calm. However, as soon as we get to our feet delusive thoughts begin to reappear one after another just as before we started sitting. This is because we stand up abruptly and roughly. The point is how to preserve the power of samadhi nurtured during meditation in the midst of activity. After many strenuous efforts in training, we will come to retain this power for longer periods, say, one or two hours. When it matures, this power makes us the master of everything wherever we might be. By emptying ourselves and plunging deeply into the surrounding world as to integrate with it, the surrounding world in turn becomes us. All oppositions cease. We treat things as they should be without being upset or without letting our minds be dispersed under any circumstances.

It goes without saying that the authentic way of zazen consists in training in the stillness of meditation and that we should sit hard and sit a great deal. The basic discipline in Zen lies in destroying again and again the oncoming delusions and worldly thoughts by applying koan and counting respiration as our sword, thus going into samadhi where Heaven and Earth are one and both mind and body are dropped. However, there are twenty-four hours in a day, and unless we practice zazen without sitting, it will be difficult to advance to the desired state of mind. . . . Talking, laughing, quarrelling, and moving the limbs should all be integrated into one and the same samadhi. If we can turn things upside down on the tops of rocks, we are superior. If we are turned upside down by things, we are inferior. . . .Zen is seeing into our own selves, realizing that we have no fixed forms, clearly seeing the no-self, and realizing its imperturbability. If we grasp this point firmly, whatever we do becomes zazen, and we are thoroughly one with everything which confronts us. When we read, we only read; when we write, we only write; when we walk, we only walk; and when we sleep, we only sleep.

Lao Tzu said, "If we learn, we gain in knowledge day by day. If we act according to the Way, we lose day by day. We keep losing until we no longer possess anything to do. In non-action we do everything." The same is true of the Way of Zen. Master Joshu said, "I entered the Buddhist life when I was a small boy. I have grown old now. Confronted with people, I now find myself powerless to save them. I used to discipline myself in order to help people some day when I became enlightened. Contrary to my expectation, however, I have become a fool whether you believe it or not." We have Zen if we become aware of nobody in need of saving when we are ready to save them. Zen is indeed without merits and without effects. But in compliance with the needs of others, the following effects have been traditionally pointed out.

> *Calmness of spirit under all circumstances*
> *Being able to choose to die while sitting zazen*
> *Realizing that every day is a fine day*
> *Acting spontaneously and without restraint*
> *Sitting alone feeling as if one were a high*
>   *majestic mountain*
> *Bringing joy to those around you*
> *Accepting any hardship*
> *Acting without concern for public recognition*
> *Seeing things as they truly are*
> *Willingness to suffer for the sake of others*

Tanouye Tenshin

In 1972 Omori transmitted his line of Zen to America with the founding of Chozen-ji in Hawaii. Given his background in fencing and calligraphy, it is natural that training at Chozen-ji integrates Rinzai practices with the martial and cultural Ways of Japan:

> At the highest level of mastery in any Way, a student enters the world of Zen. Conversely by training in Zen, a student may attain the highest level of mastery in his Way. The Ways teach a person to enter Zen through the body. For instance there is the principle of *Shin Ki Roku Ichi* which can be translated as the oneness of mind, energy, and body, or mind and body made one through breath. When this is grasped, tension and relaxation, calmness and alertness are correctly balanced. One's entire being enters the work which will exhibit graceful power and beauty whether it be a swordcut in fencing, a shot in archery, a character in calligraphy, or a bowl in ceramics. . . .One uses space, time, and energy in a manner which is beyond conscious contrivance and can only be called wondrous. For the Zen Master life itself is his art, and everything he does from routine activities to moral decisions shines with this wondrous quality.

> — *The Brochure of Chozen-ji*

65

Tanouye Tenshin is the Zen master at Chozen-ji. He was born in 1937 in Hawaii. From childhood he trained in the martial arts, particularly in Kendo, and later mastered several including Judo, Karate-do, as well as Kendo. He graduated from college with a degree in music and until 1978 taught music and the martial arts in high school. For a period of ten years he traveled to Japan every summer in search of an enlightened Kendo teacher. When he finally met Omori Sogen, he thought Omori was just another priest, and as was his custom at the time, began berating the provincial, materialistic image Japan was giving the world. Unlike others who shirked the responsibility, Omori stepped back, bowed, and said, "Forgive me. I have no excuse."

Subsequently Omori demonstrated the Hojo to him, and within it Tanouye saw the essence of the martial arts. Tanouye asked to be instructed. But only three days remained before he had to return to Hawaii, so Omori laughed and told him to come back when he had three years. But Tanouye persisted and in three days received Omori's approval.

Tanouye describes the purpose of Zen training this way:

> When a person's sense of inner achievement has become muted, he turns to the clamor of the world. Losing all sense of a living center, he is caught in the bondage of a hundred different situations. He becomes alienated from his spiritual power and tries to find fulfillment in the excitement of cheap stimuli, the satisfaction of his animal desires, or an exaggerated sense of self importance. His power to perceive true tranquility and harmony or to reconcile opposites and transcend dualism seems non-existent.
>
> Tranquility is life in its absolute form; it is an expression of life's natural harmony, a criterion of all that is worthwhile in life, and finally as a mark of life which has achieved perfection. . . .The Zen man owes his admirable ability to preserve his inner tranquility amidst the clamor of life neither to his being thick skinned nor to an originally harmonious nature, but to *shugyo* (the deepest spiritual training possible). This training leads to far more than freedom from external distraction. The source of our deepest self-consciousness, the root of our individual being which is fundamentally identical with the Universal Being is at stake. If one loses the samadhi point of view, he loses his root, his contact with Reality.
>
> A man who has been tried by life is nearer to tranquility than

one who has not gone through the school of suffering. Those who know great suffering know great truth. But tranquility can only be a dominating factor when a person comes to realize life's purpose while still in his prime, and the purpose will be found in samadhi.

Zen training and the Ways aim at the maturity of human being. Maturity means being in the state of mind which can see harmony in disharmony, unity in opposition. Human life is full of activity which becomes automatic and can only be performed perfectly through practice, but where do we find training aimed at developing the inner life and not particular accomplishments. Because a person has more or can do more does not mean that he is more. But in any pursuit besides the prospect of developing skill, apart from any specific achievement, there is a chance to broaden one's outlook and attain to a greater degree of maturity. Then a person's effectiveness comes out of his essential being. This is not due to the possession of certain abilities but the releasing and cultivating of his personal nature.

From the first experience of tranquility to living in this state is a long way. In Zen after you go through your koan training, at the end we ask you what is your *shinkyo* (your frame of mind going through life). Miyamoto Musashi said, "It is like a huge boulder rolling down hill." I say, "If you like to ride your Honda bike through life, that's okay, but I'm riding my tank." Take another example: You are in a plane and looking down the aisle. If you have an ego, your world is very small. But practice your zazen, look one hundred eighty degrees, and pretty soon you will find that the airplane is moving in you; people are walking in you. To go through life with this feeling, we do Zen training.

To introduce students to Zen, Tanouye often uses the letters Master Takuan (1573-1645) wrote to swordsmaster Yagyu Munenori (1571-1646). This collection is called the "Fudo Chi Shin Myo Roku". Fudo means immovable; chi is wisdom; shin means divined; myo is mysterious wonder; and roku is record. Together they may be translated as "The Record of Immovable Wisdom and Divine Mystery." This record can be better appreciated with some background information on Takuan and Yagyu.

Several incidents attest to Yagyu's excellence as a swordsman. Once he defended the Shogun Hidetada from a surprise attack. He slew seven men in a flash and then secreted the Shogun away as the enemy regrouped.[1] Once when watching the performance of a peerless Noh actor, he was asked by the Shogun Iemitsu, "Is the actor thoroughly alert? If he has any openings, tell me." After the play Yagyu said, "He never had an unguarded moment save for a bare instant when he rounded the corner of the pillar. Then I could have attacked him." Later the actor expressed deep admiration for Yagyu, saying, "He really is a master swordsman worthy of the name. When I turned at the corner, I relaxed my attention. Then I saw him smiling."[2]

On another occasion Yagyu was lost in the beauty of cherry blossoms radiant in soft spring sunshine when he suddenly whirled and scanned his garden intensely but saw nothing except his page holding his sword. He returned to the house and immersed himself in deep contemplation. Finally a concerned attendant asked him about his strained countenance. Yagyu replied, "When I was viewing the cherry blossoms, I suddenly felt a murderous air about me. I quickly reacted but could find no enemy. I consider it the mark of our style of fencing to perceive the opponent's intent before any actual movement. I cannot tolerate my mistaken perception." The attendants were silent when suddenly the page prostrated himself and pleaded, "Please pardon me. When I saw you captivated by the cherry blossoms, a terrible idea occurred to me. I thought that if I were to strike you at that moment, even you would not be able to parry the attack." Yagyu smiled and said, "Now I understand."[3]

Despite his attainment Yagyu did not consider himself the equal of Takuan. He wrote:

> The Mind. . . .is. . . .Emptiness itself, but out of this Emptiness an infinity of acts is produced: in hands it grasps, in feet it walks, in eyes it sees, etc. This Mind must once be taken hold of, though it is indeed very difficult to have this experience because we cannot get it from mere learning, from the mere listening to others talk about it. Swordsmanship consists in personally going through this experience. When this is done, one's words are sincerity itself, one's behavior comes right out of the Original Mind emptied of all ego-centered contents. The mind we generally have is defiled, but the Original Mind is pure—the Tao itself.
>
> I talk as though I have experienced all this, but really I am far from being a Tao-man. I note it down simply because all human life ought to be in conformity with this view of the Mind. If we are still unable to apply it to every phase of our life, as swordsmen we must have it at least in the exercise of our art.[4]

The difference between the sword master and the Zen master is further illustrated below.

Once Shogun Iemitsu, Yagyu, and Takuan were admiring a wild tiger when the Shogun suggested to Yagyu that he use his fencing ability to approach the tiger and stroke its head. Despite the warnings of the tiger's keeper, Yagyu entered the cage. Holding a fan before him, he fixed his gaze on the tiger and slowly advanced. The tiger growled threateningly, but Yagyu managed to hold it at bay and just touch its head. Slowly he retreated, and as he came out sweat poured off him. The Shogun turned to Takuan and said, "Has Zen anything else to show?" Takuan ran down to the cage, his sleeves flying in the wind, and jumped in. Facing the tiger, he spat on his palm and held it out to the tiger which sniffed then licked his hand. Takuan lightly touched its head, then turned and softly jumped out of the cage. "After all," marvelled the Shogun, "our way of the sword cannot compete with Zen."[5]

The following are excerpts from a lecture by Tanouye on Takuan's letters to Yagyu. It was given to a group of Zen students at an intensive training session at the Chicago branch of the Chozen-ji. Takuan's writings are indented with Tanouye's commentary appearing as text in the following pages.

THE RECORD OF IMMOVABLE WISDOM
AND DIVINE MYSTERY

1. *Mumyo Juchi Bonno*

Mumyo means absence of light; it is also called *mayou* which is delusion. In Kendo we have four admonitions: Number one, you must overcome fear. The second one says you must overcome suspicion. The third is not to be taken by surprise or to be taken aback. And the fourth is not to have delusions. Actually it's all fears. The reason you practice Kendo is to take away these four. Now when that happens, for the first time you have attained to the Way in Kendo. Juchi means dwelling place; and bonno means evil passions. Mumyo juchi bonno refers to affective disturbance at the dwelling place of ignorance. In other words, when you have an absence of enlightenment, you're going to dwell, and at that dwelling place of ignorance, you have affective disturbances in your mind. The first letter goes this way:

To dwell is the same as to stop; to stop means that the mind attaches itself to a particular thing. In swordsmanship, for instance, when the opponent tries to strike you, your eyes at once catch the movement of his sword; and you may strive to follow it. But as soon as this happens, your mind stops on the opponent's sword. Your movements will lose their freedom, and you will be killed by your opponent. This is what I mean by stopping.

Although you see the sword about to strike you, do not let your mind stop there. Do not intend to strike him by according his rhythm. Cherish no calculating thought whatsoever. You perceive the opponent's move but do not allow your mind to stop with it. You move on *sono mama*, just as you are, enter, and wrench the enemy's sword away. Then the sword meant to strike you will instead become the sword which will strike the enemy.

Here's what we do: We say, "Okay, we won't let our minds stop on the sword." But you see the rhythm; he's coming; you're going to accord with the rhythm and get him. Takuan is saying don't even think that. You see but don't react. Don't let it stop you; move on just as you are. But just imagine a guy is wild, and he's coming for you. Your mind's going to stop. So to go in and wrench the sword away is not an easy thing.

This is the same as *Muto* (no sword) which is highly esteemed in swordsmanship.

In Kendo the highest principle is Muto. Now if you have a sword in your hand, it can still be Muto. Muto is the void sword. What is this sword? It's a koan in itself. What is the void? What is Mu? If you really know the void, I tell you, "Then without using your hands make me stand up!"

2. *Shobutsu Fudo-chi*

Shobutso means all Buddhas; fudo means immovable; and chi is wisdom. Shobutsu fudo-chi is the immovable wisdom of all Buddhas.

Although fudo means immovable, it is not the immobility or insensibility of inanimate things like a stone. It is the mind capable of infinite movement. It can move forward and backward, left and right, to every direction in the ten quarters and knows no stopping anywhere. Immovable wisdom is this mind.

What does he mean? When you're looking for a fly in the room, are you stopping on anything? All of a sudden the fly crosses your mind, then you focus on it and stop. You cannot see the whole room anymore. Why do you do that? Because you want to get the fly.

There is a Buddhist statue called Fudo Myo-O. He holds a sword in his right hand and a rope in his left. His teeth are bared, and his eyes glare penetratingly. He dynamically stands to destroy the evil spirits or demons who try to harm or hinder the Buddha's teachings. . . .He embodies immovable wisdom for all sentient beings to see.

The enemy of Buddhism is delusion. If you look at the statue long enough, you can become Fudo Myo-O and meditate with that feeling. It takes that kind of willpower to cut off your delusions. The Fudo Myo-O that I like the most is by Miyamoto Musashi. In his later years he carved one in the *basso kamae* (a Kendo stance) with a sword. It's a beautiful thing.

In Vietnam people burnt themselves up to protest the war. How were they able to do that? A monk would say, "On a certain day at a certain time at a certain intersection, I'm going to burn myself up." He goes there, pours gasoline on his body, and enters the fire samadhi, the Fudo Myo-O. He strikes the match, and he burns soundlessly with a peaceful expression on his face. If you become enlightened and carry your life as exemplified by Fudo Myo-O, you will not be touched even by evil spirits.

Fudo Myo-O is the unmoving One Mind of everyone. . . . Immovable means not to stand still with whatever object one encounters. Not to move means not to stop. . . .If the mind stops with each object, it will be disturbed by thoughts. This will lead to the movement in the heart. . . that is disturbance. Therefore, there will be no freedom of movement.

This is difficult to understand. If you stop and your mind is moved from place to place because of your attachments, you actually have no freedom of movement. You stopped on one thing.

For example, suppose ten men are ready to strike you with a sword. *Ukenagasu* (parry) the first without your mind stopping. Forget that man and encounter the next, and in this way all will be dealt with successfully. . . .Ten men, ten separate encounters without the mind stopping on any, and all will be successively and successfully dealt with. But if your mind stops with the first, although you may be able to ukenagasu his sword, with the second man you will inevitably fail.

The only English word for ukenagasu is parry, but we never parry in fencing. When you block with a sideward movement, it's not natural, and there's nothing but flaws. So you ukenagasu the first man without your mind stopping. Forget him, encounter the next, and the next, and so on. This is very important: ten men, ten encounters. You're facing ten men in practice. You throw the first guy down. "Oh, that wasn't too good." Your mind stopped. That's not right now; it's the past already. Then you worry about the guy coming to you. He didn't even come yet; that's the future. Right there is the problem of life! Taking it moment by moment, this is how we should live.

Kannon Bosatsu (the Bodhisattva of Compassion) is sometimes represented with one thousand arms each holding something different. If his mind stops with the use of one, all the other nine hundred ninety-nine arms will be of no use. . . .The figure demonstrates that when immovable wisdom is realized, even as many as one thousand arms on one body may all be used efficiently.

You ever watch a drummer? You ever wonder what a conductor goes through? At times you beat time here, a different time with your feet, a different time with your hand. How are you going to do that?

The beginner knows nothing about the ways of holding a sword nor concern for himself. When the opponent strikes, he instinctively struggles without calculation. But as soon as his training starts, he is taught how to hold the sword, where to place his mind, and many other techniques which make his mind stop at various places. Thus he loses his freedom of movement.

As days, months and years go by, as his training acquires fuller maturity, his bodily attitude and his way of handling the sword advance toward no-mindness, which resembles the state of mind he had at the very beginning when he was all together ignorant of the art. When the highest level is reached, body and limbs perform what they have learned by themselves with no conscious effort. . . .The mind does not dwell; where the mind is, is not known. . . .In the same way when one reaches the highest stage in Buddhism, a man turns into a kind of simpleton who knows nothing of the Buddha, nothing of his teachings, and is devoid of all scholarly acquisitions.

3. *Honshin Moshin*

Honshin is your Original Mind or your True Mind. Moshin is the deluded mind.

> The Original Mind is the mind which does not stop but pervades the whole body and being. . . .When the Original Mind is fixed on a particular thing, it is called the deluded mind and will fail to function anywhere. . . .The Original Mind is like water which flows freely, whereas, the deluded mind is like ice with which one cannot even wash hands and feet.

Let's say you're going to sit zazen. Just after you settle down, you aren't thinking about anything. You're just ready. Why don't you stay like that? It's difficult, right? The next thing you know you're thinking, "Oh, the pain in my knee. It's getting itchy. It's getting cold." All kinds of thoughts occur. One method to deal with them is just before they emerge, put strength in your hara "Ummph" and cut them short. Another method is to let them come and go, just don't give them any fuel. For instance, a car is going "rrrm." "A car. . . ." Stop. That's it. Let it go. Next, "Oh, I'm hungry." Leave it alone. Pretty soon it peters out, appears and disappears. But if you cling to thoughts, for instance, "I'm hungry. Boy, I wish I had a piece of steak in front of me. I can just taste it. And a bottle of sake on the side. After this training I'm going down to the bar and drink up", that's bad. That's moshin. But remember when you just got into position, at that point you have your Original Mind. It's very important to keep that mind.

Now you may not have faith in that Mind, but all creative intuitions come from it. Let's say you have a problem and can't get the answer. You work at it, you work at it, you build up the tension. All of a sudden you're sitting on the toilet, and there it comes. Or you might lie down to sleep, and all of a sudden get the answer, the "Aha!" feeling. What happened is you gave up and weren't thinking. So you got back to your Original Mind, and all of a sudden you got the solution. The Original Mind tends to look at things as a whole, whereas, the deluded mind tends to be very partitive.

4. *Ushin Mushin*

Ushin is the conscious mind; mushin is no-mind or void mind.

The conscious mind is the deluded mind. One can read the characters as a mind conscious of itself. In everything it is one-sided. The mind with thoughts in it will give rise to discrimination and wavering. It is also called the dichotomous mind. . . . Mushin is not rigid or one-sided. At the time when there is no discrimination, thought, or anything in the mind, the mind will pervade the whole body and being. . . .There is a poem:

> *To think that I am not going to think of you*
> *is still thinking of you.*
> *Let me then try not to think that I am not*
> *going to think of you.*

Necessarily your conscious mind works in dichotomy, yes against no, up against down. A whole school of Chinese philosophy teaches us there's no such thing as up and no such thing as down, no such thing as big and no such thing as small. Things which exist in relation to something else are not real.

There's a koan: "Thinking neither good nor evil, what is your Original Face at that time?" If you think yes—no, black—white, subject—object, all these opposites, when you're doing that, what are you doing? What is the Original Face? What's in between the two. Think of it. Try saying to yourself, "Yes—no, yes—no." What's in between? You say it's empty space. But there's still someone watching that. When you really realize what it is, you can have your yes—no and still be your Original Nature.

5. *Motomu hoshin, Shin Yo Ho*

This is a saying of Mencius which means to bring the runaway mind back to our being but not to stop or leave it there.

Bring the runaway mind back to the tanden, (the center of being, traditionally located two inches below the navel), but don't let it stop there. The minute you say, "Now it's there," it stopped. The tanden "Over here. Over there. On my toe." I can put my tanden any place I want to. Why? Because the whole Universe is like a ball, and any point in the ball is the center of the Universe. I am the center of the Universe. You are the center of the Universe, too, if you really real-

ize this. But to train ourselves in the beginning, we develop the
tanden. Later on if you can let all your feeling just settle right down
into your tanden, your whole body will become empty. There will be
no inside and outside. This is why I can say this is the tanden, this is
the tanden, or this is the tanden. But if we just say this from the
beginning, you wouldn't know where to turn. For instance, we have
this beautiful mountain in Hawaii called Haleakala. It's terrific; it's
really nice; it's very windy; it even snows up there. If I describe how
terrific it is, but I don't tell you how to get there, what are you going
to do? You'll say, "Oh, that was an interesting story." But if I say
you catch the direct flight to Honolulu. Get off, transfer to the plane
for Maui. Borrow a car at the U-drive, and just follow the arrows
saying Haleakala. It points all the way up. This is all method. But
after you get there, don't stop at Haleakala. It's too cold. Come back
down again. When you reach the top, the ideal from your religious
point of view, you must come back down. Otherwise you're like a
mental patient who goes to the hospital to cure himself, and after
he's cured, he stays in the hospital. He's really nuts. In other words
you're just like a hermit. We say you stink of Zen.

If anything, now you know that there is a definite method to bring
you to a certain frame of mind. The only thing stopping you is your
weakness to continue. You can see where the mountain goes to. I'm
telling you the tanden is here; it's a terrific thing. Okay, the mountain is steep; the road is straight up; and we're going to start climb-
ing. If you walk one step at a time without thinking anything, just
one step at a time, like crawling up a mountain, eventually you'll get
there. But many people climb for a while, then they stop, look at the
top, and say, "Wow, it's really far." They climb a little more and say,
"Oh, I can't make it," and give up. But if you keep going, when you
reach the top, you'll find that the top was the bottom of the mountain. All it took was one step.

ZEN
THERAPY

❖

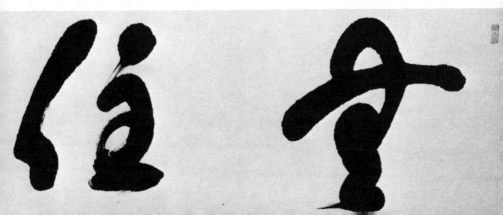

From galaxies to atoms, from bodies to thoughts, all things are energy fields of varying degrees of permanence, power, and clarity. There is a formless, cosmic, sentient energy which has been called different names throughout history and across cultures, for examples: *shakti, chi, ki, mana*, and spirit. This vital energy is the subtlest manifestation of the Way.

It evolves into increasingly sophisticated forms in order that existence may see itself. With the evolution of the ego, the capacity for self-reflection and thus the possibility of Nature fulfilling itself has been attained. To realize this possibility, the ego must be transcended. This is the end of Zen Therapy.

The Way:
A Philosophy of Life

We are responsible for our experience of circumstances. Circumstances may be beyond our influence, but our experience can be free and boundless under any circumstances. This was demonstrated by Daito Kokushi, who lived among the beggars, and even more vividly by Kwaisen, the abbot of Yerin-ji who in 1582 refused to hand over soldiers seeking refuge at his temple. He and his monks were locked in a tower which was then set ablaze. In their usual manner they sat in zazen, and the abbot gave his last sermon, "We are surrounded by flames. How would you revolve your Wheel of Dharma at this critical moment?" Each then expressed his understanding. When all were finished, the abbot gave his view, "For peaceful meditation, we need not go to the mountains and streams. When thoughts are quiet, fire itself is cool and refreshing." They perished without a sound.[1] This is the power of the Way.

As a philosophy of life, the Way upholds self-realization as the highest good and deepest pleasure. Without maturation a person's life remains shallow and unfulfilling. But the Way focuses on self-realization through the cultivation of vital energy rather than reasoning. Reasoning cannot answer the existential need of human being: the need for meaning that can withstand even senseless suffering, the need for communion amidst turmoil, and the need for fulfillment in the face of death. Reasoning does not enable one to live in the manner of Kwaisen and his monks. For this vital energy must be cultivated until human being vibrates at a higher level and experiences the oneness of the universe. As Hakuin wrote:

> If you distill it (the vital energy) over the years, protect it to the utmost, and nourish it constantly, then before you know it the elixir-oven and the whole universe becomes a mass of this great circulating elixir. Then you will awaken to the fact that you yourself are a divine sage with true immortality, one who was not born before heaven and earth was formed and who will not die after empty space has vanished.[2]

Samadhi can be conceptualized as the free flow of vital energy both within the body and between the body and the universe. Kaneko Shoseki, a Japanese healer, gave the following description of what might be called the "metaphysiological" dynamics of vital energy.

> By *keiraku* I mean those imperceptible fine passages in the body which connect bones, muscles, brain, intestines, the senses, etc. with each other and eventually reconnect them all with the primal Life Force. Like the blood vessels and nerve fibers connecting all the inner organs, they run through the whole body, mostly alongside the blood vessels. . . .Their function is in the nature of supervising the circulation of blood and movement of thought and allowing each organ to work harmoniously with all the others. . . .They are so to speak a network of passages which transmits to all parts of the body the spiritual-physical rhythm of the Life Force. . . .
> Only through calm, deep breathing can the primal Life Force preserve its actual function in rhythm with the eternal Being, and the keiraku receives its power and transmits it to each separate part of the body. This is the essential condition not only for perfect health but also for true knowledge. . . .
> Practice every day, let go all your fixed notions and feelings, indeed let go completely your present I. When through long serious practice you shed all preconceptions, become inwardly clear and empty you will gradually be able to delay exhalation for quite a long while and to retain the breath in the lower belly deeply and quietly. When this happens the strain of wrong effort will gradually ease, inner perception will grow clearer and in the tanden you will feel a source of strength never before experienced--the Original Source.
> Apart from the normal communication between men through

language and action there is another quite different sort of mutual influence. It is that of the rhythm of the Original strength which permeates all human beings and all Nature. Through it every individual thing in essence and, as it were, underground is connected with every other. If then one who is further removed from the working of the Primordial Force is close to one who lives more in accord with it, the rhythm of the Primordial Force will certainly be transmitted from the one to the other. The latter without knowing it exerts a good influence on the other.

The relation between artistic creation and the tanden is immediate and essential. Neither the hand nor the head should paint the picture. It is an expression of the essential in all art, the artist must empty and free his head, and then concentrate his whole energy in the tanden. His brush will then move of itself in accord with the rhythm of the Primordial Force. If, on the contrary in drawing the lines, he uses the strength of his hand or if he works under personal tension, what he wants to express will be cut off from the source of inner synthesis and will look hard and fixed.[3]

Breathing in rhythm with the pulsation of the universe is the basic practice of the Way. Thoughts and feelings are difficult to grasp, but a person can train the musculature to refine breathing and attain to what Taoists call embryo breathing.

When the practitioner achieves embryo breathing, he is said to be in the state of total extinction, or cessation. It is the primordial beginning of the universe. In man it is referred to as breathing without breath. This is called embryo or primordial breathing. From it man draws the invisible, ungraspable force of the universe for compounding the elixir of vital energy.[4]

To achieve embryo breathing is to abide in Tao.

Way is a translation of the Japanese *Do* which in turn is a translation of Tao. A distinctive achievement of Japanese culture was to transform fighting skills such as fencing (Kendo) and archery (Kyudo), as well as routine activities such as serving tea (Chado) and arranging flowers (Kado) into Ways. Ways are formalizations of Tao in specific fields of activity. They are art forms for disciplining the spirit and refining breath, posture, and awareness. Practice of a Way leads to the cultivation of vital energy. Ultimate mastery of a Way consists of the realization of the true Self when vital energy reaches a critical level of intensity and clarity.

Because any activity can be used for self-development, a person can find meaning and fulfillment in the perfection of one's role, whatever it may be. A story from Chuang-tzu illustrates.

> *Prince Wan Hui's cook*
> *Was cutting up an ox.*
> *Out went a hand,*
> *Down went a shoulder,*
> *He planted a foot,*
> *He pressed with a knee,*
> *The ox fell apart*
> *Without a whisper.*
> *The bright cleaver murmured*
> *Like a gentle wind.*
> *Rhythm! Timing!*
> *Like a sacred dance.*
> *Like "The Mulberry Grove,"*
> *Like ancient harmonies.*
>
> *"Good work!" the Prince exclaimed,*
> *"Your method is faultless."*
> *"Method?" said the cook*
> *Laying aside his cleaver,*
> *"What I follow is Tao*
> *Beyond all methods!*
>
> *"When I first began*
> *To cut up oxen*
> *I would see before me*
> *The whole ox.*
> *All in one mass.*
> *After three years*
> *I no longer saw this mass.*
> *I saw the distinctions.*
>
> *"But now I see nothing*
> *With the eye. My whole being*
> *Apprehends.*
> *My senses are idle. The spirit*
> *Free to work without plan*
> *Follows its own instinct*
> *Guided by natural line,*
> *By the secret opening, the hidden space.*
> *My cleaver finds its own way.*
> *I cut through no joint, chop no bone.*

"A good cook needs a new chopper
Once a year—he cuts. A poor cook needs a new one
Every month—he hacks!

"I have used this same cleaver
Nineteen years.
It has cut up
A thousand oxen.
Its edge is as keen
As if newly sharpened!
True, there are sometimes
Tough joints. I feel them coming,
I slow down, I watch closely,
Hold back, barely move the blade,
And whump! The part falls away
Landing like a clod of earth.

"Then I withdraw the blade,
I stand still
And let the joy of the work
Sink in.
I clean the blade
And put it away."

Prince Wan Hui said,
"This is it! My cook has shown me
How I ought to live
My own life." [5]

A Way consists of principle (*ri*) and techniques. The principle is
formlessness or abiding in the Tao. Techniques are forms which
were once spontaneous expressions of principle by a master. By per-
fecting form through countless repetitions, a person attains to formlessness. Then a person accords with the myriad changes naturally.
Without principle, technique is mechanical; without technique, principle cannot be expressed. With both technique and principle, there
is grace.

The ego is a form which has been developed over countless generations of life. It is a technique for living in a civilized manner.
Zen training transcends the ego by mastering it. A person learns to
endure pain and austerity, delay gratification, concentrate fully on
the task of the moment, each moment, and refine form to the nth
degree. Training ends with losing the ego and realizing the freedom
of the true Self.

In the practice of the Way, nothing is gained. Rather unnatural fixations ranging from muscular tension, immature attitudes, to vicious circles of interpersonal interactions are lost. In Lao Tzu's words:

To learn,
One accumulates day by day.
To study Tao,
One reduces day by day.
Through reduction and further reduction
One reaches non-action,
And everything is acted upon.
Therefore, one often wins over the world
Through non-action.
Through action, one may not win over the world.[6]

Eugen Herrigel's account of his Kyudo master's shooting illustrates non-action.

"I think I understand what you mean by the real, inner goal which ought to be hit. But how it happens that the outer goal, the disk of paper, is hit without the archer's taking aim, and that the hits are only outward confirmations of inner events—that correspondence is beyond me."

"You are under an illusion," said the Master after a while, "if you imagine that even a rough understanding of these dark connections would help you. These are processes which are beyond the reach of understanding. Do not forget that even in Nature there are correspondences which cannot be understood, and yet are so real that we have grown accustomed to them, just as if they could not be any different. I will give you an example which I have oftened puzzled over. The spider dances her web without knowing that there are flies who will get caught in it. The fly, dancing nonchalantly on a sunbeam, gets caught in the net without knowing what lies in store. But through both of them 'It' dances, and inside and outside are united in this dance. So, too, the archer hits the target without having aimed—more I cannot say."

(This, however, did not quell Herrigel's doubts, so the Master invited him to come to the practice hall one night.) The practice hall was brightly lit. The Master told me to put a taper, long and thin as a knitting needle, in the sand in front of the target, but not to switch on the light in the target-stand. It was so dark that I could not even see its outlines, and if the tiny flame of the taper had not been there, I might perhaps have guessed the position of the target, though I could not have made it out with any precision. The Master 'danced' the ceremony. His first arrow shot out of dazzling brightness into deep night. I knew from the sound that it had hit the target. The second arrow was a hit, too. When I switched on the light in the target-stand, I discovered to my amazement that the first arrow was lodged full in the middle of the black, while the second arrow had splintered the butt of the first and plowed through the shaft before embedding itself beside it. I did not dare to pull the arrows out separately, but carried them back together with the target. The Master surveyed them critically. "The first shot," he then said, "was no great feat, you will think, because after all these years I am so familiar with my target-stand that I must know even in pitch darkness where the target is. That may be, and I won't try to pretend otherwise. But the second arrow which hit the first— what do you make of that? I at any rate know that it is not 'I' who must be given credit for this shot. 'It' shot and 'It' made the hit. Let us bow to the goal as before the Buddha!"[7]

When the parameters of a person's model of reality are empty space, linear time, and causality through local energy exchanges between independent bodies, then the phenomenon of "It" shooting is impossible to grasp. When the parameters are interpenetration, the absolute present, and synchronicity, a person is then effective on a more implicate order of reality where there is no subject and object; thus the master expresses his experience in terms of It shooting. But It shot by virtue of his training in the Way.

In Japanese culture the creative process is described in terms of *ki* (vital energy), *kan* (transcendent intuition), and *myo* (wondrous action). Tanouye Roshi once thought of opening a school of fencing with the motto, "Ki ga kan o ataeba, myo no oto ga deru." (When energy strikes intuition, a wondrous sound emerges.) When energy is intense and clear enough, transcendent intuition works, and wondrous action emerges. Wondrous action is mysterious, synchronous, and creative; Suzuki has a particularly poetic description of myo.

> *Myo* is a certain artistic quality perceivable not only in works of art but in anything in Nature or life. The sword in the hands of the swordsman attains this quality when it is not a mere dis-

play of technical skill patiently learned under the tutorship of a good master, for myo is something original and creative growing out of one's own unconscious. The hands may move according to the technique given out to every student, but there is a certain spontaneity and personal creativity when the technique, conceptualized and universalized, is handled by the master hand. *Myo* may also be applied to the intelligence and the instinctive activities of various animals, for example, the beaver building its nest, the spider spinning its web, the wasp or ant constructing its castles under the eaves or beneath the ground. They are wonders of Nature. In fact, the whole Universe is a miraculous exhibition of a master mind and we humans who are one of its wonderful achievements have been straining our intellectual efforts ever since the awakening of consciousness, and are daily being overwhelmed by Nature's demonstrations of its unfathomable and inexhaustive *myo*. The awakening of consciousness has been the greatest cosmological event in the course of evolution. . . .The function of human consciousness, as I see it, is to dive deeper and deeper into its source, the unconscious. And the unconscious has its strata of variable depths: biological, psychological, and metaphysical. One thread runs through them, and Zen discipline consists in taking hold of it in its entirety, whereas other arts, such as swordsmanship or tea, lead us to the comprehension of respectively particularized aspects of the string.[8]

Five different levels of mastery in the Way are described in the following Kendo story.

A swordsman was annoyed by a rat in his house and sent his pet cat after it. But the rat bit her, and she ran screaming away. The swordsman then hired some neighboring cats. Crouching in a corner, the rat watched them approach and furiously attacked them one after another. The cats were terrified and all beat a retreat. The swordsman became desperate and tried to kill the rat himself, but the rat dodged his sword so skillfully it seemed to be flying in the air.

As a last resort, he sent for a famous Cat widely known for her mysterious virtue in catching rats. She did not look out of the ordinary, but when the rat saw her coming, it became terrified and could not move. The cat approached slowing and quietly, seemingly unaware of anything unusual, almost nonchalantly went for the rat, and came out carrying it by the neck.

In the evening the Cat was honored by the other cats. They bowed deeply and said, "We are all noted for valor and cunning, but none of us could do anything with that rat. Yet how easily you carried the day. We all wish you would tell us your secrets, but before that let us see how much we know about the art of fighting rats."

A black cat came forward and said, "Since I was a kitten I have trained to become a great rat-catcher. I can leap over a screen seven feet high; I can squeeze myself through a tiny hole the size of a rat; I can make them think I am sleeping and strike them when within reach. I am ashamed I had to retreat before that old rat today."

The Cat said, "What you have learned is the technique of the art. Your mind is ever conscious of planning how to fight the opponent. Those who simply imitate the masters and rely on manipulatory skill may be efficient and achieve the highest degree of technical cleverness, but what does it all amount to? When the Way is neglected and mere cleverness aimed at, training is misguided and apt to be abused."

A tiger cat now stepped forward and expressed his view. "I consider ki (vital energy) most important. I have cultivated it over the years and now possess spirit that fills heaven and earth. When I face an opponent, my spirit overawes him, and victory is won before the actual fighting. I have no conscious scheme as to the use of techniques, but it emerges spontaneously according to changing situations. I can make a rat running over a beam fall by gazing at him with my spiritual strength. But that mysterious rat moved without a shadow; the reason is beyond me."

The Cat replied, "You can make the most of your psychic power. But because you are conscious of it, your psyche stands opposed to the opponent, and you can never be sure of being stronger. You may feel as if your active, vigorous psyche filled the universe, but it does not. It may resemble Mencius' *Kozen no ki* (the vital energy of the universe), but in reality it is not. Mencius' ki is bright and illuminating and for that reason full of vigor, whereas yours gains vigor owing to conditions. The one is a great river incessantly flowing, and the other is a temporary flood after a heavy rainfall, soon exhausted by a mightier onrush. For a cornered rat the fight is for life and death, and the desperate prey harbors no desire to escape unhurt. Its mental state defies every possible danger; its whole being incarnates the fighting ki, and no cats can withstand its steel-like resistance."

A gray cat advanced quietly and said, "For a long time I have disciplined myself not to overawe the enemy, not to force a fight, but to yield and simply follow up his movements. I act like a curtain surrendering itself to the pressure of a stone thrown at it. Even a strong rat finds no means to fight me, but the one today had no parallel."

The old Cat answered, "What you call a yielding psyche is not in harmony with Nature; it is man-made, a contrivance worked out by your conscious mind. When you try to crush the opponent's positive, impassioned, attacking psyche, he will detect any wavering in your mind. Artificially evoking the yielding psyche produces a certain degree of muddiness and obstruction in your mind, which surely interferes with acuteness of perception and agility of action. Nature is impeded in pursuing its original and spontaneous course.

"To make Nature display its mysterious way of achieving things is to do away with all your own thinking, contriving, and acting. Let Nature have her own way, let her act as it feels in you, and there will be no shadows, no signs, no traces whereby you can be caught, no foes who can resist you. . . .But there is one essential point: Do not cherish even a speck of self-conscious thought. If this is present in your mind, all your acts become self-willed, human-designed tricks and do not accord with the Way. Then people refuse to yield to your approach and oppose you. When you are in mushin (void mind), you act in unison with Nature without resorting to contrivances. The Way, however, is beyond limitations, and all my talk far from exhausts it."

"Some time ago in my neighborhood was a cat who passed all her time sleeping and looked like a wooden statue. People never saw her catch a single rat, but wherever she roamed there were no rats. I once visited and asked the reason. She gave no answer. I asked four times, but she remained silent. It was not that she was unwilling to answer, but in truth did not know how to answer. So we note that one who knows speaks not, while one who speaks knows not. That old cat was forgetful not only of herself but of all things around her. She was in the highest spiritual state of purposelessness. She was a divine warrior and killed not. I cannot compare with her."[9]

The five levels in this story are: 1. the use of physical technique, 2. the use of vital energy, 3. yielding, 4. according to nature, and 5.

abiding in Tao. The black cat was at the first level, and the tiger cat at the second. At both these levels the awareness of fighting an opponent dominates. The gray cat with his practice of the yielding psyche was at the third. He was trying to transcend technique and be like the cat who was natural, for whom rats were just cats' food. The cat at the highest level was one with Tao and beyond words.

The Transcendent Unconscious
and the True Self

When all is said, Zen discipline consists in realizing the
Unconscious which is at the basis of all things, and this Unconscious is no other than Mind-only in the *Gandavyuha* (Kegon
Sutra) as well as in the *Lankavatara*. When Mind is attained not
as one of the attainables but as going beyond this existence dual-
istically conceived, it is found that Buddhas, Bodhisattvas, and
all sentient beings are reducible to this Mind, which is the
Unconscious.[1]

—Daisetz Suzuki

The Unconscious Suzuki speaks of is the transcendent Unconscious, the deepest and highest state of awareness which transcends
the duality of conscious and unconscious. The metapsychology of
the *Lankavatara Sutra*, which Bodhidharma said contained "the
essential teachings of the Buddha concerning his mental ground,"
articulates nine structures to describe the development of consciousness. These are the five senses (*vijnanas*), the intellect (*manovijnana*),
the ego (*manas*), the storehouse unconscious (*alayavijnana*), and the
transcendent Unconscious (*adarsanajnana*).

This system is set in motion by the karmic memories impressed
in the storehouse unconscious. Suzuki wrote:

91

Psychologically *vasana* is memory, for it is something left after a deed is done, mental or physical, and it is retained and stored up in the storehouse unconscious as a sort of latent energy ready to be set in motion. This memory or habit-energy, or habitual perfuming is not necessarily individual; the storehouse unconscious being super-individual holds in it not only individual memory but all that has been experienced by sentient beings. When the Sutra says that in the storehouse unconscious is found all that has been going on since beginningless time systematically stored up as a kind of seed, this does not refer to individual experiences, but to something general, beyond the individual, making up in a way the background on which all individual psychic activities are reflected.[2]

Suzuki describes the workings of this system in the following manner:

In the beginning there was the memory amassed in the storehouse unconscious since the beginningless past as a latent cause, in which the whole universe of individual objects lies with its eyes closed; here enters the ego with its discriminating intelligence, and subject is distinguished from object; the intellect reflects on the duality, and from it issues a whole train of judgements with their consequent prejudices and attachments, while the five other senses force them to become more and more complicated not only intellectually, but affectively and conatively. All the results of these activities in turn perfume the storehouse unconscious, stimulating the old memory to wake while the new one finds its affinities among the old.[3]

If we all thought of the storehouse unconscious as external and subject to changes, we must now retrace our steps and look within ourselves and see if there is anything that transcends the principle of particularization. To transcend the principle, that is, for the ego and the intellect to transcend themselves, means the obliteration of themselves, their disappearance from the field of operation, the transcending of the dualism of. . . one and many, particularity and generality. When this is accomplished, where do we find ourselves? Where is the ultimate abiding place for us?[4]

When all these limits are transcended—which means going even beyond the so-called collective unconscious—one comes upon what is known in Buddhism as *adarsanajnana* (the transcendent Unconscious), "mirror-knowledge". The darkness of the unconscious is broken through and one sees all things as one sees one's face in the brightly shining mirror. (Parenthesis mine.)[5]

The transcendent Unconscious refers to a level beyond the storehouse unconscious. It is not a structure, but a transformation of the whole system into wisdom.

1. The storehouse unconscious becomes the great, perfect, mirror-wisdom.
2. The ego becomes the wisdom of equality.
3. The intellect becomes the wisdom of wondrous perception.
4. The five senses become the wisdom of wondrous workings.[6]

A less metaphysical interpretation of the system is possible in terms of cognitive development. The nine structures distinguish five modes of cognition: perception, apperception, rationality, intuition, and wisdom. Each mode integrates the information of lower ones in a more comprehensive understanding. Since they differ qualitatively, each mode suggests a distinct developmental stage: the baby, the child, the adult, the mature adult, and the true Self.

COGNITIVE STRUCTURE	COGNITION	DEVELOPMENTAL STAGE
Five Senses	Perception	The Baby
Intellect	Apperception	The Child
Ego	Rationality	The Adult
Storehouse Unconscious	Intuition	The Mature Adult
Transcendent Unconscious	Wisdom	The true Self

The One Mind in Buddhist metapsychology can be conceived of as formless, sentient energy evolving into increasingly sophisticated and unitary systems of awareness in order to see itself. In human being reflexive awareness and with it the possibility of Mind realizing itself has been attained. In the course of evolution certain memories have been impressed on human being. These memories are energy structured into patterns of varying complexity and immutability. The five senses are fixed in the genes of the human race. The intellect as the capacity to order basic sensations into a world view is a more complex but still pervasive phylogenetic structure. The ego is even more sophisticated and is an inherited structure only in modern human being. Reflexive awareness makes ego development possible, and the ego provides the viewpoint from which Mind can recollect itself as always having been only Mind. The ego is realized in the course of normal development in the modern person; the real challenge is to realize the storehouse and transcendent Unconscious and leave these memories as a contribution to the human race.

Perception refers to sensations unordered by concepts. Out of an infinite reality, the five senses access stimuli of a certain kind and range. Stimuli are pristine, undifferentiated chaos for the baby after birth. In the womb the baby and the environment are one. After birth the first major differentiation made by the baby is between the environment and the self fused with the mother. The next, between the self and the mother, comes from the repeated experience of deprivation and gratification of physiological needs.

Apperception is the ordering of perception by the intellect according to the world view of one's society. By highlighting aspects important to survival and deleting others, the world view enables human being to function in an otherwise overwhelming reality. The intellect executes more abstract logical operations with maturity, but its primary function in childhood is to order experience according to the dualistic categories of the ordinary world. Hence in Buddhism it is sometimes considered another sense along with the five basic ones.

> (The world of particular objects) comes in contact with the five senses, and all the impressions gained from this contact are presented to the intellect which is sort of a door-keeper between the ego and the five senses. All the impressions and reports gathered at the intellect are here classified according to the categories of "me and not-me".[7]

Rationality measures reality with dualistic, linear thinking which assumes the ego as its point of reference. It is the standard for adult behavior in modern society. Although rationality and the ego are milestones in phylogenesis, in personal development they are only techniques applicable at a certain level, which a person must master and be free of. When one clings to rationality and the ego as final realities, one is trapped in the phenomenal world of memories taking form according to his attachments and cannot transcend the suffering inherent in dualism.

Intuition discerns reality by tapping the storehouse unconscious. The storehouse unconscious may be considered the implicate order of reality as found in the human mind. When a person reaches the limits of rationality but remains focused on his problem, the problem like a koan sinks into the storehouse unconscious which contains all possibilities. Then resolution emerges spontaneously. For the mature adult struggling with existential questions or the artist striving to perfect his art or the scientist seeking a breakthrough, the only way out is in. The following examples of Nobel prize-winning physicist Enrico Fermi and the haiku poetess Chiyo illustrate this.

> I will tell you how I came to make the discovery (about the effects of slowing the neutron beam through paraffin) which I suppose is the most important one I have made. We were working very hard on the neutron induced radioactivity and the results we were obtaining made no sense. One day, as I came to the laboratory, it occurred to me that I should examine the effect of placing a piece of lead before the incident neutrons. And instead of my usual custom, I took great pains to have the piece of lead precisely machined. I was clearly dissatisfied with something: I tried every "excuse" to postpone putting the piece of lead in its place. When finally, with some reluctance, I was going to put it in its place, I said to myself, "No, I do not want this piece of lead here; what I want is a piece of paraffin." It was just like that: with no advance warning, no conscious prior reasoning. I immediately took some odd piece of paraffin I could put my hands on and placed it where the piece of lead was to have been.[8] (Parenthesis mine)

> Wishing to know what a true haiku was, Chiyo visited a master and was given the cuckoo as a subject. She composed several haiku, but the master rejected them all as conceptual and not true to feeling. Not knowing how to express herself more genuinely, one night she meditated on the cuckoo so intently that she did not notice the passing of time. When dawn lit her room, the following haiku formed itself in her mind.

> > *Cuckoo, cuckoo,*
> > *All night long,*
> > *Dawn at last!*

The master praised it as one of the finest ever written on the cuckoo.[9]

Wisdom refers to the realization of the transcendent Unconscious through *prajna* or transcendent intuition. Suzuki wrote:

> Prajna's vision. . . knows no bounds; it includes the totality of things, not as a limited continuum, but as going beyond the

boundlessness of space and the endlessness of time. Prajna is a unifying principle. It does this, not by going over each individual unit as belonging to an integrated whole, but by apprehending the latter at one glance, as it were. . . .

It (the undifferentiated continuum immediately given to our consciousness) is. . . "an iron bar of ten thousand miles"; it has no "hole" by which it can be grasped. It is "dark"; no colors are discernible here. It is like a bottomless abyss where there is nothing discernible as subject and object. These statements. . . are figurative and do not give much information regarding prajna-intuition. But to those who have gone through the actual experience of prajna-intuition, these figurative, symbolic statements are really significant.[10]

Unlike intuition consisting of insights from the storehouse unconscious, transcendent intuition penetrates beyond this level and transforms the entire system into the fourfold mirror wisdom. Takuan described the functioning of such a person in this manner:

Put a mirror down somewhere. Everything that is in front of it is reflected in it, exactly as it appears. The mirror has no consciousness, is unable to differentiate, therefore it reflects things exactly as they are. The same is the case with a master in the art of conflict. He is open to the pure mirror of his spirit and is unclouded by any trace of the consciousness which separates and distinguishes one thing from another, distinguishing between good and evil. Yet his mirrorlike soul is not blind to "this" and "that," to "good" and "evil;" he sees without being forced to see. If the mirror of the soul is without consciousness, pure and free from the slightest trace of prejudice, then everything on Heaven and Earth is reflected in it, just as it is. A man who possesses such a mirror is absolutely present in perfect command of the moment and the attitude of mind which is called for at that point. . . .He and he alone can produce natural action, wonderful in that it can be subjected to every conceivable change, action without action, whether in the art of fencing or any of the arts of life, and containing in itself the wisdom of Buddha.[11]

In Buddhism the attainment of wisdom and compassion are inseparable. Compassion is a natural consequence of the realization that the true self is no self and is one with the universe. As long as the sense of the self as a separate entity remains, however, a person is fundamentally moved by anxiety about the destruction of the self.

The nature of anxiety changes from physiological, to interpersonal, economic, and existential with the identification of the self with progressively deeper and wider systems. This development is outlined below.

DEVELOPMENTAL STAGE	MOTIVATION	SELF-IDENTITY
Baby	Physiological	Body
Child	Interpersonal	Family and Peers
Adult	Economic	Society
Mature Adult	Existential	World
True Self	Compassion	Universe

Self-development involves a continual interplay of homeostasis, stress, and anxiety. Homeostasis refers to the psychophysical balance of the self between changing internal and external demands. Samadhi can be operationalized as a perfected homeostasis changing according to changing conditions. Stress refers simply to the energy needed to adapt to these changes; the more vital energy a person has, the better one is able to adapt and grow with changes.

Stress is inescapable because as the first Noble Truth states, existence is impermanent. Anxiety, however, can be transcended; anxiety is experienced when the self feels threatened by excessive change. Anxiety is termed mind-stopping in Zen; basically the mind stops because of attachment to the self. When the self is threatened, the energy rises; the shoulders tighten; breathing is restricted; and the field of experience closes in.

Much stress and probably some anxiety accompany the transition between developmental stages. But in healthy development stress serves as a stimulus to further maturation, and anxiety is outgrown as new cognitive structures and self-identifications are realized. A higher homeostasis is established, freeing energy for further growth. In impaired development a significant amount of energy is constantly being depleted to repress anxiety not resolved at lower levels. This creates a vicious circle as new internal and external demands which could lead to further growth, lead instead to more anxiety, ineffectiveness, repression, and finally to collapse.

A baby experiences the self as the body. When physiological homeostasis is upset, the baby cries. In healthy development physiological needs are well met, and basic trust is established.

A child identifies with the self seen through the eyes of first the family and then the peer group in school or the neighborhood. A child must maintain not only a physiological but also a psychological homeostasis dependent on fluctuations in the child's self-esteem in interpersonal relationships. The task is to learn the social order.

An adult must maintain economic viability in the general society not only for oneself but often for children. An adult's experience of self extends to the community one lives and works in.

A mature adult extends the identification of the self to the world. In modern times a global perspective is necessary, given the economic interdependence of nations and the power to destroy the world through nuclear war. A mature adult faces the bewildering social and political problems in the world. Trying to understand them leads to the questioning of the meaning of existence itself.

At the most mature level of human being, a person realizes the true Self which is one with the universe and experiences a meaning beyond question and articulation. Such a person transcends anxiety, is fearless, and is moved by compassion.

Wisdom, compassion, and fearlessness are ultimately one, but the line of Chozen-ji emphasizes fearlessness. Tanouye Roshi says that to give fearlessness is the highest act of compassion. The following story about Yamaoka Tesshu illustrates.

> A young fencer who asked him about the inmost secret of the Way of fencing was told to go to the Kannon Temple at Asakusa and pray to be given enlightenment about it.
>
> After a week the man came back and said, "I went every day and prayed for a long time but nothing came in response. But as I was coming away yesterday, for the first time I noticed what is written above the shrine: *The Gift of Fearlessness*. Was that what you meant?"
>
> "It was," replied Tesshu. "The secret of our Way is complete fearlessness. But it has to be complete. Some there are who are not afraid to face enemies with swords, but who cringe before the assaults of passions like greed and delusions like fame. The end of our Way of fencing is to have no fear at all when confronting the inner enemies as well as the outer enemies."[12]

Creative Problem Solving

Therapy is the art of problem solving. Problems arise when one attaches to forms which block the natural course of vital energy and stifle growth. These forms may range from aberrations in the body, rigid attitudes, simple routines, addictions, ineffective patterns of communication, and ultimately the ego itself. When a person transcends form and lives from an enlightened perspective, every day is a fine day. Zen Master Mumon wrote:

> *Hundreds of flowers in spring, the moon in autumn,*
> *A cool breeze in summer, and snow in winter;*
> *If there is no vain cloud in your mind*
> *For you it is a good season.*[1]

Problem solving at its most creative occurs when the Zen master utters the turning words which free the disciple from dualism, as when Bodhidharma told Hui-ke, "Bring your mind, and I will pacify it," or when Hui-neng told Mieng, "Think neither good nor evil. What is your true Self?" The intervention works not because of the meaning of the words. Lin-chi may have shouted, "Katsu!" with the same results. Tao working through the emptiness of the master transforms the being of the disciple. When samadhi prevails, nothing is lacking in the responsive activity of the unconscious.

There are many stories in Zen about masters helping people with their problems which can easily be seen as masterpieces in psycho-therapy. For example:

A woman sought help for a phobia. She and her husband had been very poor, but through hard work and good fortune they were now prosperous and needed to entertain for the sake of their business. But for fear of losing it all, she could not bring herself to spend the money necessary.

After talking with her awhile, the master asked her to teach him the game of "paper, scissors, stone" which she had been expert in as a child. In this game paper wraps stone, stone breaks scissors, and scissors cuts paper. Paper is made by opening the hand, stone by closing the fist, and scissors by pointing the middle and index fingers out. They started to play but the master kept making stone, and it was no contest. She explained the game again, but now he kept making paper. Finally he just said that this game was beyond him and walked away, leaving the woman bewildered.

The woman went home, puzzled over it all day, and when her husband came home, began to tell him the story. Laughingly she acted out how the master kept making stone and then paper. As she was making paper, she stopped, stared at her hand, and then made stone and looked at that. She became lost in thought.

After she was able to entertain generously without spending money wastefully. She had learned what she already knew. Keeping the fist closed or keeping the hand open, penny pinching or extravagance both were counterproductive.[2]

Compare this story to the following two clinical cases from Milton Erickson and Nick Cummings respectively.

(A fourteen year old girl had become pathologically reclusive because she feared her feet were too large. She refused to dis-cuss her problem.) I arranged with the mother to visit the home . . .under false pretenses. The girl would be told that I was com-ing to examine the mother to see if she had the flu. It was a pretense, and yet the mother wasn't feeling well, and I suggested that an examination would be appropriate. When I arrived at the home, the mother was in bed. I did a careful physical examina-tion of her, listening to her chest, examining her throat, and so on. The girl was present. I sent her for a towel, and I asked that she stand beside me in case I needed something. She was very concerned about her mother's health. This gave me an opportunity to look her over.

Studying the girl, I wondered what I could do to get her over this problem. Finally I hit upon a plan. As I finished my examination of the mother, I maneuvered the girl into a position directly behind me. I was sitting on the bed talking to the mother, and I got up slowly and carefully and then stepped back awkwardly. I put my heel down squarely on the girl's toes. The girl, of course, squawked with pain. I turned on her and in a tone of absolute fury said, "If you would grow those things *large* enough for a *man* to see, I wouldn't be in this sort of situation." The girl looked at me, puzzled, while I wrote out a prescription and called the drugstore. That day the girl asked her mother if she could go to a show, which she hadn't done in months. She went to school and church, and that was the end of a pattern of three months' seclusiveness. I checked later on how things were going, and the girl was friendly and agreeable. She didn't realize what I had done, nor did her mother. All her mother noticed was that I had been impolite to her daughter when I visited that day.[3]

Kate was referred to me by a Jungian analyst who had been seeing her for three years. His hostility was so great that he disqualified himself from treating Kate who was a schizoholic. He warned that she would come in drunk one session, would urinate in his chair the next, and finally would do some semblance of therapeutic work the third. The sessions alternated among those three behaviors but he would never know whether or when Kate would urinate. To ward off the consequences of this, before Kate came in he always put a rubber sheet over the therapy chair, the kind you use in a baby's crib. He also told me that all attempts to stop this symptom resulted in Kate's falling to the floor, stopping breathing, becoming cyanotic, and turning blue, at which point he would have to call the paramedics to come in and resuscitate her and literally save her life. At this point I had to assume certain educated risks. I became an authority on cyanosis during the next couple of weeks before I saw her. She had spent the time becoming an authority on me. She had very cleverly pumped her previous therapist about what kind of guy I was and in order to justify his sending her to me he told her, "I'm a very, very easygoing, kind man. Nick Cummings is tough; he's a tough s.o.b." So Kate came in anticipating my behavior.

True to her expectations I said, "Kate, the first time you urinate in my chair ends our therapeutic relationship." She looked at me and without saying a word, she cleared her throat and spat on my carpet. I handed her the box of Kleenex and said, "Kate, clean it up." She replied, "You didn't tell me I couldn't spit on your carpet." I said, "Kate, I don't intend to tell you a lot of things that I know your mother taught you not to do. I'm not going to tell you that you shouldn't squat in the middle of the boulevard that's in front of my office and urinate. I'm not going to tell you a lot of things you already know. But I am telling you that kind of behavior is out." She stared at me without a word for three or four minutes, stopped breathing, and began to turn blue.

Instead of calling the paramedics, I did what I prepared and started fumbling in my desk for my camera. I discovered, much to my dismay, that my camera was empty. I started fumbling for film, all the while saying, "Kate, keep that up. It's fantastic. We're going to make medical history with this. I've got to take pictures of this." I completely unravelled the first roll of film before I got it into the camera. I reached for another roll of film, all the while pleading, "Kate, keep this up. Please, Kate." Every once in a while Kate would open one eye and stare up at me in total disbelief. Finally, when I got the camera loaded and began to take pictures, my flash didn't work so I started fumbling around with the flash. Before I could get the flash attached and functional with a new battery, Kate was back in her chair saying, "Oh, you!"

Kate was known in every emergency room of every hospital in San Francisco. She would fall to the floor in the waiting room and become cyanotic. After our fourth session I got her permission to give my name and number to each emergency room next to her name. So when Kate appeared in the middle of the night in an emergency room, I got called. I only went down once. As I came down the hall, I could hear her gasping as she turned blue. I called out, "Alright Kate, get up!" I heard, "Oh, Dr. Cummings." By the time I got to the waiting room, she was up sitting in her chair, and the blueness was leaving her face. After the first time, I did this by phone. I instructed the emergency room attendant merely to hold the phone up to Kate's ear. I would yell over the phone, "Alright Kate, up!" I would hear Kate say, "Oh, you!" as she would get up. The baffled intern would come on the phone and say, "What did you do?" I'm happy to say that within three weeks Kate stopped this symptom.

By the time Kate and I terminated on the 18th session, she had gone from looking like Apple Annie to a self-respecting human being. She started to groom herself and stopped drinking. She was still schizophrenic, but she was no longer a schizoholic who had to go through life getting attention by becoming cyanotic or urinating in therapists' chairs.[4]

The creativity and effectiveness exhibited by these examples come from self-development and not the learning of any form. Milton Erickson and Nick Cummings had unique life experiences which forced them to be their own first clients. Various models have been constructed upon their work. Here the focus is on the life experiences that led them to practice therapy as a way of life.

Milton Erickson

From birth Erickson coped with color blindness, arrhythmia, tone deafness, and dyslexia. He could only see the color purple. His heart beat irregularly. He had a tendency to reverse letters and words. These constitutional problems kept his worldview more flexible than normal, and the acquisition of ordinary precepts was a memorable insight for him. For example, he could not distinguish between a "3" and an "m," until one day the teacher took his hand and wrote a "3" and then an "m." Erickson reminisced:

> Can you imagine how bewildering it is? Then one day, its so amazing, there was a sudden burst of atomic light. I saw the m and I saw the 3. The m was standing on its legs and the 3 was on its side with the legs sticking out. . . . There was a blinding flash of light and in the center of that terrible outburst of light were the 3 and the m . . . .I saw them as they were.[5]

At seventeen Erickson suffered a severe attack of polio which forced him beyond ordinary limits in order to survive. He described the crisis of the illness as follows:

> As I lay in bed that night I overheard the three doctors tell my parents in the other room that their son would be dead in the morning. I felt intense anger that anyone should tell a mother her boy would be dead by morning. My mother then came in with as serene a face as can be. I asked her to arrange the dresser, push it up against the side of the bed at an angle. She did not understand why, she thought I was delirious. My speech was dif-

ficult. But at that angle by virtue of the mirror on the dresser I could see through the doorway, through the west window of the other room. I was damned if I would die without seeing one more sunset. If I had any skill in drawing, I could still sketch that sunset. I saw that vast sunset covering the whole sky. . . .I saw all the sunset but I didn't see the fence and large boulder that was there. I blocked everything except the sunset. After I saw the sunset, I lost consciousness for three days.[6]

Immobilized in bed after the attack, Erickson was functionally a participant-observer to the interactions of eight siblings, two parents, and a nurse and began to grasp the intricacies of communication.

Although I already knew a little about body language and other forms of non-verbal communication, I was amazed to discover the frequent, and, to me, often startling contradictions between the verbal and non-verbal communications within a single interchange. This aroused so much of my interest that I intensified my observations at every opportunity.

The discovery that "double takes" were perceptions at two different levels of understanding, often based upon totally different experiential associations, opened a new field of observation. Then, when I discovered that a "triple take" could occur, I began mentally rehearsing the phrasing of a single communication to cause differing perceptions, even contradictory in character, at different levels of understanding. These efforts led to the recognition of many other factors governing communication such as tonalities, time values, sequences of presentation, near and remote associations, inherent contradictions, omissions, distortions, redundancies, over-and-under emphases, directness and indirectness, ambiguities, relevancies and irrelevancies—to name a few. Also, it became apparent that there were multiple levels of perception and response, not all of which were necessarily at the usual or conscious level of awareness but were at levels of understanding not recognized by the self, often popularly described as "instinctive" or "intuitive."[7]

Despite the prognosis that he would never walk again, Erickson recovered mobility by evoking childhood memories of movement and painstakingly bringing the normally unconscious workings and relationships of the relevant psychophysical systems into awareness. By reinforcing his impaired sensations over and over with the energy of his attention, Erickson succeeded in making his body functional again. This practice led to an acute kinesthetic sense and great sensitivity to nonverbal communication.

> I lay in bed without a sense of body awareness. I couldn't even tell the position of my arms or legs in bed. So I spent hours trying to locate my hand or my foot or my toes by a sense of feeling, and I became acutely aware of what movements were. Later, when I went into medicine, I learned the nature of muscles. I used that knowledge to develop an adequate use of the muscles polio had left me and to limp with the least possible strain; this took me ten years. I also became extremely aware of physical movements and this has been exceedingly useful. People use those little telltale movements, those adjustive movements that are so revealing if one can notice them. So much of our communication is in our bodily movements, not in our speech. I've found that I can recognize a good piano player not by the noises he makes, but by the way his fingers touch the keys. The sure touch, the delicate touch, the forceful touch that is so accurate. Proper playing involves such exquisite physical movement.[8]

After his first year at the university, Erickson completed his rehabilitation in the summer by canoeing up and down the rivers of the Midwest. At the beginning he was unable to pull his canoe out of the water, to swim more than a few feet, and to paddle more than a few miles downstream. His resources for the summer were a small sack of beans, another of rice, and $2.32. He fished, found edible plants along the river, and scrounged among the peelings dumped by steamboat cooks for whole potatoes or apples included by mistake. Occasionally he would work for a day. He studied a German book to prepare for medical school. He canoed from June to September and travelled 1,200 miles. By the end of summer his rehabilitation was impressive. He could carry his own canoe, swim a mile, and paddle upstream against a four mile current from dawn to dusk. In 1952 Erickson suffered a rare second attack of polio which markedly affected his right arm and side. Within a year he made a difficult hike in the Arizona mountains with the use of two canes.

Erickson described problems as the "roughage" in life. Accepting and making the most of them meant life could be thoroughly enjoyed. He wrote:

> Psychotherapists have a wrong idea about sickness, handicaps, and death. They tend to overemphasize the matter of adjustment to illness, handicaps, and death. There is a lot of hogwash

going around about assisting families in grieving. I think you ought to bear in mind that the day you were born is the day you start dying. And some are more efficient than others and don't waste a lot of time dying, and there are others who wait a long time. . . .I try to impress upon patients: "Enjoy life and enjoy it thoroughly." And the more humor you can put into life, the better off you are.[9]

Erickson died in 1980 leaving behind case upon case of brilliant psychotherapy. In one dramatic case he gave ten more years of life to a man paralyzed by stroke and wasting away.

A woman in California wrote to me that her husband was totally paralyzed as the result of a stroke and could not talk. She asked if she could bring him to me. It was such a pitiful letter that I agreed, thinking that I might be able to comfort the woman enough to allow her to accept her difficult situation.

She brought her husband to Phoenix, registered at a motel, and came with him to see me. I had my two sons carry the man into the house, and I took the woman into my office and talked with her alone. She said that her husband, a man in his fifties, had this stroke a year previously, and for that year had been lying helpless in a ward bed in the hospital of a university. The staff would point out to students, in his presence, that he was a terminal case, completely paralyzed, unable to talk, and all that could be done was to maintain his health until he eventually died.

The woman said to me, "Now, my husband is a Prussian German, a very proud man. He built up a business by himself. He's always been an active man and an omnivorous reader. All his life he's been an extremely domineering man. Now I've had to see him lying there helpless for a year, being fed, being washed, being talked about like a child. Every time I visited him at the hospital I'd see the hurt and utterly furious look in his eyes. They told me he was a terminal case, and I asked my husband if they had told him that, and he blinked his eyes affirmatively. That's the only means of communication he has."

As she talked, I realized that I need not merely comfort the woman; something might be done with the man. As I thought it over, here was a Prussian, short-tempered, domineering, highly intelligent, very competent. He had stayed alive with a furious anger for a year. His wife had, with extraordinary labor, managed to load him into a car, drive clear from California, drag him out of the car and put him into a motel, then take him out and put him into the car to drive to my house. My two sons had difficulty carrying him into the house, and yet this woman had moved him across country.

So I said to the woman, "You brought your husband to me to be helped. I'm going to do my level best to help him. I want to talk to your husband, and I want you to be present, but I can't have you interfering. You won't understand *what* or *why* I'm doing what I'm going to do. But you can understand my statement that you are to sit there quietly with a straight face and say nothing, do nothing, no matter what." She managed to accept that; later when she wanted to interfere, a deterrent look restrained her.

I sat down in front of the man who was helpless in the chair, unable to move anything but his eyelids. I began to talk to him in roughly the following way. I said, "So you're a Prussian German. The stupid, God damn Nazis! They thought they owned the world, they destroyed their own country! What kind of epithets can you apply to those horrible animals. They're really not fit to live! The world would be better off if they were used for fertilizer."

The anger in his eyes was impressive to see. I went on, "You've been lying around on charity, being fed, dressed, cared for, bathed, toenails clipped. Who are you to merit anything? You aren't even the equal of a mentally retarded criminal Jew!"

I continued in that way, saying all the nasty things I could, adding such points as, "You're so goddamn lazy you're content to lie in a charity bed." After a while I said, "Well I haven't had much opportunity or time to think of all the insults you so richly merit. You're going to come back tomorrow. I'll have plenty of time the rest of today to think of all of the things I want to say to you. And you're going to come back, aren't you!" He came back right then with an explosive, "No!"

I said, "So, for a year you haven't talked. Now all I had to do was call you a dirty Nazi pig, and you start talking. You're going to come back here tomorrow and get the *real* description of yourself!"

He said, "No, no, no!"

I don't know how he did it, but he managed to get to his feet. He knocked his wife to one side and he staggered out of the office. She started to rush after him, but I stopped her. I said,

"Sit down, the worst he can do is crash to the floor. If he can stagger out to the car, that's exactly what you want."

There is nothing quite like a Prussian; they can be so domineering, dictatorial, incredibly sensitive to what they consider insults. I have worked with Prussians. Their demand for respect is so great, their self-image so bloated with self-satisfaction. Here was a man who had been insulted beyond endurance for a whole year in the hospital—then I showed him what insults could really be like and he reacted.

I said to the wife, "Bring him back tomorrow at eleven o'clock in the morning. Drive him to the motel now, and drag him into his room. Put him to bed, following your previous routine of taking care of him. When it's time for him to go to sleep, as you walk out of his bedroom and into your own, tell him he has an appointment with me at eleven o'clock tomorrow. Then keep right on walking out of the room.

"Tomorrow morning feed him his breakfast and dress him. Then at ten-thirty say, 'We've got to leave now for Dr. Erickson's office.' Walk out and get the car, drive it up in front of the door, and race the engine. Wait until you see the doorknob turn. Then you can go and help your husband out and into the car."

The next morning they arrived. He walked, with only her assistance, into the office and we got him seated in a chair. I simply said, "You know, it was worth going through that hell yesterday to be able to walk out of this office. To be able to say at least one word. Now the problem is, how do I get you to talk and to walk and to enjoy life and to read books. I prefer not to be as drastic again. But you didn't believe in yourself at all. I was sufficiently unpleasant to give you no recourse except to protest. I hope now we can be friends. Let's get started on your restoration to at least some normal activity."

He was very worried in his facial expression. I said, "You realize that I can make you speak by insulting you, but I think you can say 'yes' to a pleasant question. In the light of what we've already accomplished, after your year of terrible helplessness, I think you will want me to continue helping you. You can answer, 'yes' or you can answer 'no.' He struggled and got a 'yes' out.

After two months he was ready to return to California. He limped badly, had circumscribed use of his arm, and some aphasic speech, and he could read books but only if he held the book far to the side. I asked him what he thought had helped him. He said, "My wife brought me to you for hypnosis. I always had the feeling after that first day when you got me angry, you were hypnotizing me and making me do each thing that I succeeded in doing. But I'll take credit myself for walking fifteen miles one day in the Tucson zoo. I was very tired afterwards, but I did it."

He wanted to know if he could return to work, at least part time. I told him he would need to list the most simple things he could do in his place of business and content himself with doing those. He agreed to that.

I received letters from her and from him periodically for nearly seven years. They were happy years. The correspondence came at greater and greater intervals, and finally it ceased. Then about ten years after their visit, his wife wrote that her husband had again had a stroke and he was badly handicapped. Would I be willing to see him again to restore him to physical health?

Considering his age, I didn't think I could possibly take him. I wrote to her and pointed out that he was past the age of sixty, and he had been badly damaged by the first stroke. Now the second one had left him unconscious for several days. He was as helpless as he had been before. I told her I didn't think there was anything more I could do.[10]

Erickson's genius in psychotherapy can be attributed in part to his phenomenal skill in verbal and non-verbal communication. But he upheld unconscious functioning as even more important and most effective both in life and therapy. He conceived of hypnotic trance as an altered state of awareness in which the habitual frameworks and limitations of the ego are depotentiated, and experiences and abilities existing in the unconscious are used to solve problems. He wrote:

> It is very important for a person to know their unconscious is smarter than they are. There is a greater wealth of stored material in the unconscious. We know the unconscious can do things, and it's important to assure your patient that it can. They have to be willing to let their unconscious do things and not depend so much on their conscious mind. This is a great aid to their functioning. So you build your technique around instructions that allow their conscious mind to withdraw from the task and leave it all up to the unconscious.[11]

> You go into autohypnosis to achieve certain things or acquire certain knowledge. When do you need that knowledge? When you have a problem with a patient, you think it over. You work

out in your unconscious mind how you're going to deal with it. Then two weeks later the patient comes in, and you say the right thing at the right moment. But you have no business knowing it ahead of time because as surely as you know it consciously, you start to improve on it and ruin it.[12]

At the present time if I have any doubt about my capacity to see the important things, I go into a trance. When there is a crucial issue with a patient and I don't want to miss any of the clues, I go into trance. . . .It happens automatically because I start keeping close track of every moment, sign, or behavioral manifestation that could be important. And as I began speaking to you now my vision became tunnel-like and I saw only you and your chair. It happened automatically, that terrible intensity, as I was looking at you. The word terrible is wrong; it's pleasurable.[13]

Nick Cummings

Like Erickson, Cummings is a master therapist. Also like Erickson, he overcame seemingly impossible problems in his personal life and demonstrates a creativity in his work that cannot be conveyed through formal training. What follows is an edited transcript of an interview with me in 1984 in Honolulu in which he described significant influences in his development.

When I was four years old, I woke up in the middle of the night with everybody screaming and crying, and found out my father had died. He was only thirty-five. My maternal grandmother came in and said, "You're the man of the house." I was four years old, and I remember how terrified I was about that.

When I read how people are prepared for a certain role in life, I know what they mean because my grandmother prepared me to be the man of the house starting at four years old. Everything she taught me was responsibility. But it was always something I could handle. She never asked me to do something I couldn't. When she felt that I could do it, there was no stopping her whether it took her one hour, one week, one month. She never let go until I did it.

I was without a father for three years. They tell me my father and I were very close. I remember just snatches of him. My father's death was kind of tragic. We were on vacation at Palm Springs. He came down with appendicitis, but it wasn't diagnosed. They called the resort doctor who didn't even come out and said to take three ounces of castor oil. He did and by three o'clock in the morning his appendix had burst. In those days there was no treatment for peritonitis. This spread all through the abdomen, and he died shortly thereafter. For three years I was without a father. I didn't even have a mother because she was in this terrible depression. So my grandmother was kind of like mother and father.

Then my mother married my stepfather. I swore he'd never take my father's place. That only lasted about six months, and then I was crazy about him. But he was an incredibly exacting taskmaster. What he required of me was unbelievable. He always told me, "I don't care what you become. I don't care if you become a ditchdigger or a poet or a businessman, as long as you're the best. If you become a ditchdigger, you better dig the fastest and best ditches in the world. If you do that, I will hit the first man the puts you down for becoming a ditchdigger. But you better become the fastest and best ditchdigger in the world. I don't care what you become." He really meant this. So all my life I've tried to meet that principle.

I was paralyzed twice in my life once at four and once at nine. When I was four, I was on a horse. Someone smacked the horse which took off in a gallop, and I caught my neck in a clothesline and broke it. When I was nine, I had polio. At four my memory is fuzzy, but I was old enough to remember many of the details of polio at nine. I remember the doctors and nurses were talking over my bed. One of the doctors said, "If this boy survives, which I don't think he will, I think he'll be dead within twenty-four hours, but if he survives he'll never walk." I remember that pissed me off, and I survived. But the pain was like someone had put a vise on every one of your muscular joints, not just like your elbows or your knees but your wrist joints, your knuckles, your ankles, your toes, and they were just tightening these vises. The pain just wouldn't abate. It just kept getting worse and worse for three days. I was determined I was going to live, and I did live.

This was during the real bad polio epidemic that the United States had in 1932 and 1933. I was in Children's Hospital in Oakland in this huge ward of kids who had polio. Once I got through my first three days, I became the guy who entertained the whole ward. I used to tell stories. I was in an iron lung for about six months and then in bed for another three months. They used to prop me up, and I would tell stories to the kids. The kids would laugh, and I'd make up stories. My grandmother was a great story teller, and I told all the stories I had heard from her. She had an incredible zest for life and a sense of humor. The kids loved these stories. I invented children's soap operas which would be continued the next day. All night long while I was lying in bed, I would write the next episode of this scenario I was telling. The kids would wake up and want to hear the rest, but I'd say they had to wait till ten o'clock after we'd had breakfast, been bathed, done our exercise, and all these things. Then I would tell them the next episode. The nurses caught on to this and would say, "If you don't let us bathe you and do the exercise, you won't get to hear Nick's story."

Finally it came time to go home, and I wanted to walk out of there. But they said, "No, you're going to go home in an ambulance." I was furious at this. So the doctors examined me, put me in a wheelchair, and wheeled me to the ambulance. My mother, stepfather, and the doctor rode home with me. They carried me upstairs. The doctor examined me again, and I was waiting for all these people to get out of there so I could walk. Finally they all left the house except my mom who had to do some chores. I said, "Now!" Somehow I got my legs over the side of the bed, pushed myself off the bed with my hands, and my legs were like jello. I just fell flat on my face. Then the terror struck. I realized I was paralyzed. I was paralyzed from the waist down. The terror really struck. My mother heard me fall, and she ran in.

I could hear my mother crying every night in bed, talking to my stepfather. She was told I'd never walk. She used to feel very guilty. She said, "God, I feel terrible. I'm asking God to forgive me because I was told my son wouldn't live, but he lived so I should be grateful. But he can't walk." I said, "Damn it, I'm going to walk." I would crawl when my mother was busy in another part of the house from my room which was like on a half story. I learned to crawl on my belly like a snake down the stairs and get into the garage. I would chin myself on a series of water and gas pipes along this wall. I would get myself on my bike. I would go out on my bike, and I would push down from my waist because my legs were worthless. I'd ride that bike. If I hit something or fell down, I'd be helpless. I'd lie there till somebody came to pick me up. I worked up to where I could go fifty miles on this bike. I used to go from my home in Piedmont which was quite hilly clear out to the Oakland Airport and back. My mother would be absolutely terrified. She would beg me, "Please don't sneak out of the house and do this. You're never going to walk again. Don't, don't torture yourself." She'd have the police looking for me. Sometimes I'd be gone for hours. It took me two years to learn to walk by riding a bike.

After I graduated from college, I was accepted to medical school, but World War II came around, and the Army decided things for me. I was put in the infantry. I joke and I say that I went on one thirty-five mile forced march too often, so when they put a notice up saying that the army was forming a new kind of combat unit called paratroopers, I volunteered. I kid and use the excuse that jumping out of airplanes has to be better than marching thirty-five miles, but the real reason was that if I was going to be a soldier, I had to be the best soldier. So at eighteen I became a paratrooper in the 82nd Airborne.

In the early part of the war, I was parachuted with fifty-seven men into Yugoslavia. We hooked up with Tito. Three days after we jumped my captain and both my lieutenants were killed. I was a staff sergeant and became the commander-in-chief of the American expeditionary force in Yugoslavia. We were there for several weeks, and I followed Marshall Tito. He was about fifty years old then, and he used to go straight up a mountain carrying a Browning automatic rifle and about fifty pounds of other equipment. I was nineteen at the time, and I could hardly keep up with him. The whole reason we parachuted in there and fought with Tito and the partisans was to show Tito that the Americans were supporting him rather than the Chetnicks. Out of the fifty-seven of us that went in there, eleven of us got out. We had to find our way from the mountains, down to the German lines to the coast to make contact with a submarine that was supposed to pick us up. Eleven of us finally got on the submarine. This was typical of what the 82nd was asked to do. I think every mission the 82nd Airborne was sent on was a suicide mission. They never expected us to come back. The average in the 82nd was three combat jumps before you got it. I made eleven. I finally got it in Bastogne.

More than 40% of our battle casualties were psychological. Eventually I became a combat officer and was sent to the School of Military Neuropsychiatry where I took a crash six month course in psychotherapy. We took some tremendous risks in those days, and the rewards were incredibly and unbelievably real. I think that's when my first experience in brief therapy came. When one of my paratroopers froze at the jump door, I had two choices. To get him out the right way by helping him to jump, or to have the jump sergeant do the usual procedure of placing his boot in the man's back and pushing him out the door. Very often when that happened, before the man hit the ground he would be in a state that I would call excited catatonia. As he landed, he would expose himself. He would run around and shoot aimlessly. That man would usually be dead five minutes after he hit the ground. So I literally had fifteen seconds to say something to get him to jump on his own before the jump sergeant would intervene and push the man out. I had a chance to do follow-up to that brief visit when he hit the ground. There I had something like thirty seconds to talk to them. That's about the briefest therapy I've done in my career but some of the most rewarding. I can honestly say that I did not lose a single paratrooper to psychoneurosis in all the time that I did brief intervention.

I've had to kill. I've had to kill several times during that period. It's a very, very difficult thing. Looking back on it, I think it was harder for me to kill than to die. I really had to struggle with that, but it had to be done. It literally had to be done. My guilt feelings. . . life has a way of taking care of things because after I was wounded with three fifty-caliber bullets in my abdomen and one in my knee and laid in the snow for three days, the war should have been over for me. But I heard that my outfit was chosen to liberate Buchenwald. The Allies were not getting into Germany fast enough, and Hitler had given the order to exterminate all Jews before the Allies reached the concentration camp. I was a captain by then, so when I heard that my outfit was going to parachute into Buchenwald, I literally walked out of the hospital. I told the colonel there that the only way he was going to stop me from leading my outfit into Buchenwald was to courtmartial me. When we parachuted into Buchenwald, they were killing the Jews so fast they couldn't bury them fast enough. There were huge trenches, and they were pushing the bodies in with bulldozers. You could smell the stench of decaying bodies way up in the air. When we got there, the survivors all looked like toothpicks. That's when I lost all my guilt feelings. Some people do have to be exterminated in order to save life. If Hitler had won the war, there would have been millions of more people killed. He would have literally killed everybody he didn't like, cripples, Jews, anybody who was handicapped.

Graduate school was very rough for me. I used to sit there and listen to my fellow students intellectualizing. I'd say "Geez, what's wrong with me? I'll never be a psychologist. I can't think like they do. I can't talk like they do. I can't spout out the stuff like they do. There's something wrong with me." But I just came to the conclusion that I have to be what I am. If it doesn't work out, I'll leave psychology and try something else. But it worked out.

After graduate school I began analytic work and was amazed that when I was given my first clients, before I could see the client, there would be an intake worker who has determined eligibility, there would be another intake worker who got all of the history, there would be a medical examination, and there would be a neurological examination. By the time I saw the client, I had a three inch thick chart on my desk that I had to read. I was told this was the right way, and the way I did it in the military probably had done more damage than good. For many years I labored under the misinformation that brief psychotherapy was not the real stuff, and I became a dedicated, practicing, orthodox analyst, the type that used to consider three hundred hours of psychotherapy as the warm up.

When I was in analytic training I was fortunate enough to get as my training analyst Erik Erickson who in those days was not respected by anyone in the Analytic movement. The Neo-Freudians claimed he was something else, and the traditionalists claimed he was Neo-Freudian, and on and on it went. Now everybody claims Erik Erickson. I was in treatment with him for about ten months. Then one day he said to me, "Well, we're going to go one more month. Then your therapy is over." I came off the couch. I was furious. I said, "What do you mean? This is the warm-up. I haven't even started my analysis." He said to me, "You're a perennial adolescent. If we stop now, you'll maintain that and do great things in life. If we keep on going, you're going to turn into a stodgy stuffed shirt. I won't be able to stand you, and I'll be ashamed that I did this to you so we're going to stop." I said, "I want another analyst. I refuse." He said, "Fine. Get another analyst if you want, but the blood won't be on my hands. With me you're through." So before our termination date, I was reconciled to quitting. I remember all my fellow analysands at that time were saying, "Oh, Nick will never amount to anything. He hasn't been analyzed. The poor guy got that terrible Erik Erickson."

During my analytic training, I also knew Frieda Fromm-Reichman. She was a remarkable person. She used to wear this beat up white coat because all good doctors in those days wore white coats. She used to have the pockets stuffed with candy. She used to go around giving schizophrenics candy. She's the one from whom I learned that delusions occupy time and space, and there's only room for one person. So if the therapist gets into it, the patient has to get out of it. This was all in the days before tranquilizers, and the patients used to do awful things. They'd defecate in the middle of the floor. She'd find a patient playing with his feces, and she'd put on rubber gloves and get down on the floor and play with the patient's feces. The patient would stop. The patient wouldn't do that anymore. She was a very, very warm person. She used to say that there's no such thing as a hopeless patient; there're only hopeless techniques and we have to discover new techniques.

One of Cummings' particularly striking cases involved a woman who was killing herself through somatization. Cumming's offered her a cyanide capsule instead.

I did this three times. These people were going to die of psychosomaticizing. I think a lot of people would accuse me of playing god. It's not that at all. I can't tell you how much you sweat. These people are so determined that they're going to kill themselves the long way that you have to bring them face to face with death the fast way in order to get them to want to live. You have to take the risk that they might kill themselves. I can admit that the third time is no easier than the first, not one bit easier. What was very gratifying was the psychologist who referred the third case to me said, "I think that is fantastic. I could never do it." I said, "It's your referral. You won't criticize me if I do it?" He said, "Nick, she's going to die anyway." That's the only time of the three that I actually had the support of a colleague. On the other instances I was very much alone.

This was a woman who had medical records that would've filled a whole shelf of books. She had seen every physician and been in and out of psychiatric hospitals. She came across very lucidly. Her mind was quite clear. But her schizophrenia was being acted out somatically. She was sure that there were all kinds of changes going on inside her body. She had developed a series of very painful eruptions all over her body. Pretty soon she couldn't sit; she couldn't lie down. The only thing she could do in life was stand, but finally the eruptions broke out on the bottom of her feet, and she couldn't stand either. Then she developed them on the trachia in her lungs, and started to wheeze. Doctors were putting tubes down her throat. This woman was really out to kill herself. She had this tremendous stubbornness. It was kind of a schizophrenic stubbornness where she was going to defeat her husband.

What I worked out was to put her in isolation. I explained to her that she was killing herself. I said, "You're not going to accept any of this; you're not going to believe; you're not going to hear me. Your acting out of your psychoses is so massive you're going to kill yourself." She was not to see any physicians. I arranged with the hospital that she would not be involved with the therapeutic community, in the basket weaving, in the therapy, in group therapy, nothing. Aside from the people who would come in and clean, and that kind of thing, the only person she would see was me. I would come in every Friday. One of my war souvenirs is a cyanide capsule I took off a German intelligence officer who was suppose to use it on himself. I took this cyanide tablet, and I would go in and talk to her. Then I would say, "I'm tired of this bullshit. This thing of dying slowly, of committing suicide slowly is a lot of bullshit. This is cyanide. I'm going to walk out of here. You have fifteen minutes to swallow that cyanide. Death will be almost instantaneous. You will only feel the pain briefly. You will be dead. You're trying to kill yourself. I challenge you to take it."

I would come back exactly fifteen minutes later. If she hadn't swallowed the cyanide, I'd put it back in my pocket and say, "You're a goddamn fraud. You don't have the guts to kill yourself so you're killing yourself the slow way and punishing your family and everybody around you." I would literally beleaguer her. She would say, "I'm mad at you. You have no right to talk to me this way." I said, "Fine. When I come back next Friday, you can fix me. You'll have fifteen minutes with the cyanide alone."

After six or seven weeks her trachia began to improve. It had to or she was going to die because I was not allowing anybody to put tubes down her. Every Friday I'd talk to her for fifteen minutes. Then I would walk out, and she would have fifteen minutes alone with the cyanide. Then fifteen minutes afterwards I would berate her for being a goddamn phoney. At the end of about eight months, she started to pull out of this and said to me with very, very real feeling, "I wish you wouldn't do this anymore." I said to her, "I won't do this anymore because I understand what you've just asked me to do. You don't want to die. You've made your decision." But she said to me, "No, I'm going to be honest with you. I've decided not to die, but I haven't decided yet whether I'm going to live." I looked at her and said, "I'll accept that. That's good enough. But I want to tell you that my work with you is going to try to get you to decide to live." She said, "Fair enough." So we accepted a compromise, and I didn't do the cyanide thing anymore. Today she's living a normal life.

No matter how sophisticated the models of therapy developed from the work of such therapists as Erickson and Cummings, the influence of life circumstances that forced their self-development cannot be overlooked. Self-development ultimately is the key to mastery.

Mind-Body Training

Mind-body training consists of four basic practices: zazen, hara development, circulating vital energy, and communication. These can be used to transform daily life into a way of self development.

ZAZEN

Zazen is the basic practice because it provides the easiest conditions in which to experience samadhi. Zazen can be operationalized as the perfection of stillness. It is an imitation of the form of Shakamuni under the Bo tree. Zazen releases awareness from conscious control and facilitates the lucidity and sensitivity which makes continued development in the other practices possible. In psychodynamic terms it can be said to cultivate the vital energy needed to realize higher level structures from the Unconscious. All Zen masters have practiced zazen. Yet it should be remembered that Nan-yueh mocked Ma-tsu's efforts at sitting zazen to become a Buddha by polishing a stone with his sleeve to make a mirror.

Significant physiological changes occur in a person practicing zazen. These include changes in brain waves from beta to alpha to theta, a lowered respiratory rate but increased respiratory volume, lack of habituation and reduced reaction time to a clicking stimulus, increased physical stability, and decreased muscular tension. It is also thought that the focus and pressure on the lower abdomen favorably stimulate the autonomic nervous system and circulate blood stored in the liver and spleen, thus effectively acting like a second heart.

The following instructions for doing zazen are excerpted from *An Introduction to Zen Disciple* by Omori Sogen.

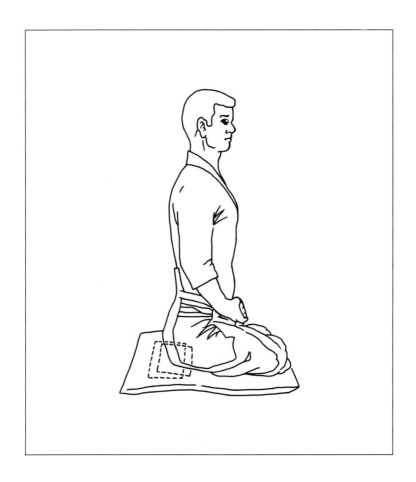

FIGURE 1
PLACEMENT OF CUSHIONS

To sit well, one must harmonize the mind, body, and breathing. Only when the
three are realized as one, will it be possible to succeed in stabilizing and
tranquilizing the body and mind at the same time. Any one of these three things
is inseparably related to the other two. If the body is correct, the mind and
the breath will be reasonably correct in themselves.

It is important to wear clothes that are loose enough for good circulation. It is
also important not to look untidy so that there is dignity in appearance and
feeling to establish the proper mood for sitting.

Select a wide cushion and two or three small ones. Stack the smaller ones
under the wide one so they act as a wedge. Sit on the edge with the buttocks off
the center of the wedge.

KEKKA FUZA
(Full Lotus Position)

HANKA FUZA
(Half Lotus Position)

FIGURE 2
THE FULL AND HALF LOTUS POSITIONS

To take the full lotus position as shown on top, place the right foot near the base of the left thigh, and place the left foot on the right thigh

To take the half lotus position as shown on the right, simply place the left foot on the right thigh or the right foot on the left thigh.

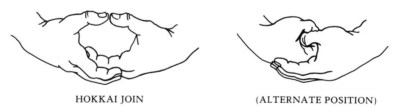

HOKKAI JOIN   (ALTERNATE POSITION)

FIGURE 3
POSITION OF THE HANDS

In the top position place the left hand with palm up and fingers together on the palm of the right hand. The inner sides of the tips of both thumbs touch, creating an ellipse. Viewed from above, the thumbs must be in line with the middle finger.

In the alternate position grasp the tip of the left thumb between the web of the thumb and the index finger of the right hand. Form a loose fist with the right hand and enclose it with the left.

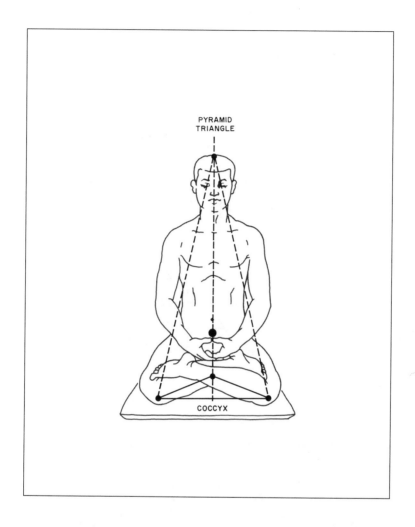

PYRAMID
TRIANGLE

COCCYX

FIGURE 4
STABILIZING THE BODY (FRONT VIEW)

A well seated and very stable body is in the form of a pyramid. The base is an imaginary triangle formed by the lines connecting the two knees and the coccyx. The diagonal ridge lines extending from the two knees and the coccyx to the top of the head complete the pyramid.

Rock the body from right to left and again from left to right. The amplitude of this oscillation should be large at first and gradually decrease until the body stops moving and becomes stable.

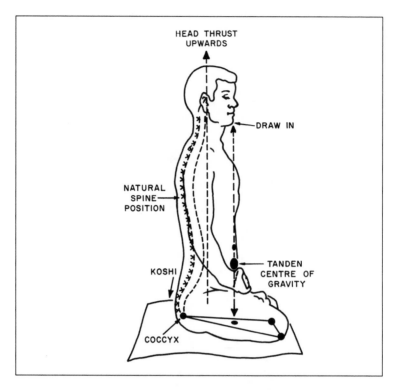

FIGURE 5
STABILIZING THE BODY (SIDE VIEW)

a. Straighten the spine perpendicularly by inclining the upper body forward. Then, push the buttocks backward without moving it while raising the upper body gradually as if to push heaven with the back of the head. This action will straighten the spine into a natural position

b. Advance the lower abdomen forward to straighten the hips. Raise the upper body until it becomes perpendicular with the neck upright and the lower jaw drawn in. The center of gravity will now coincide with the geometrical center of the plane triangle.

c. Check and see that the lower jaw is drawn in and the back of the neck is straight. If they are in the correct position, the ears and shoulders should fall in the same perpendicular plane.

d. Check also the position of the lower abdomen and the hips. If the lower abdomen is forward and the hip bone is upright, the nose and navel should be aligned.

e. Let the tip of the tongue touch the upper jaw with the teeth in light contact with each other.

f. Sit at ease, heavily and in alert dignity like Mt. Fuji soaring into heaven and overlooking the Eastern Seas.

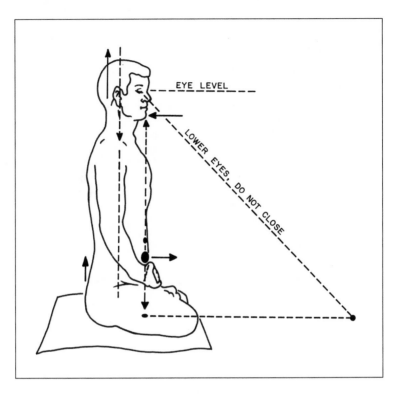

FIGURE 6
ADJUSTING THE VISION

Adjusting the vision helps to focus attention to prevent it from being taken up by internal or external stimuli.

a. The eyes should look straight ahead, and the visual field should span 180 degrees. Lower the eyes to a fixed position on the floor approximately three feet ahead. The eyes should be half-closed in selfless tranquility neither seeing nor not seeing anything.

b. Do not close the eyes. In order to enter the state of Zen concentration and to raise your inner power to the utmost, it is important to keep the eyes open. If one remains quiet with eyes closed like lifeless water, he will never be useful to society. It may seem easier to unify ourselves spiritually by closing the eyes, but then it will be inert zazen. Interpreting it more lightly, keeping the eyes open prevents us from falling asleep in meditation.

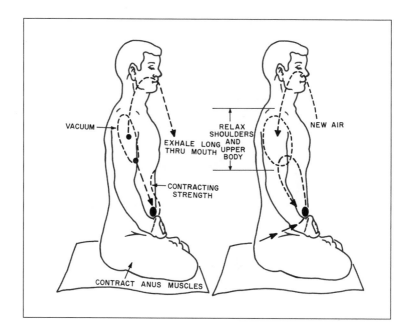

FIGURE 7
INITIAL DEEP BREATHING

Deep breathing harmonizes the mind and the body.

a. Exhale slowly through the mouth as if to connect the atmosphere with the lower abdomen. Empty all stale air with the strength created by the contraction of the lower abdomen. At the end of exhalation, relax the lower abdomen.

b. Due to atmospheric pressure, new air will naturally enter through the nose and fill the vacuum in the lungs.

c. After inhaling fully, pause slightly and with the *koshi* (*Koshi and hara* both refer to the lower abdomen, hips, lower back, and buttocks functioning as a unit. *Koshi* emphasizes the physical body, and *hara* has more spiritual significance.) extended forward, gently push the inhaled air into the lower abdomen in a scooping motion. The key to this is to contract the anus muscle.

d. Start exhaling again just before you feel uncomfortable. Repeat this type of breathing four to ten times.

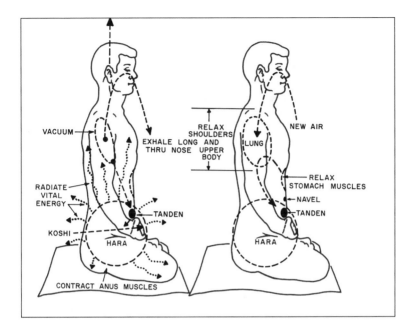

FIGURE 8
BREATHING IN MEDITATION

a. When the respiration is adjusted, start breathing through the nose with the mouth closed. Inhaling is natural through the nose. Of course the inhaled air comes to the lungs but by relaxing the muscles around the pit of the stomach, you can actually feel the air filling the area below the navel.

b. Exhale through the nose. It should be long and directed toward the tanden with the power of the abdominal muscles. Contract the muscles around the anus and push the hips upright and slightly forward. The power should feel as if coming out of the area below the navel. In the process of exhaling powerfully, the pressure on the lower abdomen recesses the stomach and relieves the pressure around the stomach area. The concentration on the lower extremities of the body should relax the shoulders and the upper body.

c. Inhaling should be left to occur naturally as new air fills the vacuum in the lungs.

d. Beginners should practice breathing with the tanden on purpose, but gradually conscious effort will lessen and the frequency of breathing will naturally decrease. In exhaling and inhaling, concentrate energy rather than physical power on the lower abdomen. When the vital power is at the tanden and confined in the *hara*, this spiritual strength and vital energy will radiate through the entire body.

e. Count your respiration with all of your spiritual power as if trying to penetrate to the core of the earth. Count the frequency of the exhalation from one

to ten. Count in syllables as long as the exhalation. O. . . . . .ne.
T. . . . . .wo. And so on. Let your mind's eye follow the exhaled
air in counting. If you miscount before reaching the count of ten or count beyond
ten, start again from one.

f. In order to avoid incongruence between your respiration and the count,
it is essential to concentrate your mind on the count rather than on the respiration
as such, and feel as if you are breathing in accordance with the count.

Precautions

Beginners tend to overstrain the area of the lower abdomen
because of the emphasis put on this area. Each individual is different in his physical structure and so must guide himself
accordingly. One should sit in such a way as to cause his energy
to pervade the whole body instead of forcing himself to put physical pressure on the lower abdomen. Only after long experience
in the practice of zazen can one comprehend the difference
between spiritual and physical power. The truth is only in the
state of Mu; one is brought into the state of emptiness through
diligent concentration of the power of the whole body at the
tanden and simultaneously infusing the whole body with the vital
energy radiating from there.

As zazen is not a test of quiet endurance, it is meaningless to
sit for long periods without concentrating and unifying the mind
and body. Thirty or forty minutes which is the time one incense
stick takes to burn is adequate for beginners. Of course five or
ten minutes will be enough if we sit fully and seriously. The crucial point is the degree of concentration rather than the length
of sitting.[1]

HARA DEVELOPMENT

Fundamentally, hara development discipline consists of correct
posture and breathing in daily activity. Refining posture and breathing
cultivates vital energy and deepens samadhi. An extremely high
level of refinement is possible. Sato Tsuji, a contemporary Japanese
philosopher, offers the following guidelines:

To achieve the right posture one must fill the lower belly
with the strength of the whole body. To fill the *koshi* (the base
of the trunk) with strength means to tense the abdominal mus-

cles a little. If one tenses them in the right way, there appears, as a result of this tension, a point of concentration below the navel. This point is the center of man as a human-body-unity. It is called the tanden. The art of activating it is to release the strength of all the other parts of the body and to concentrate it there. . . .

Filling the koshi with strength goes naturally hand in hand with breathing out. While inhaling one must withdraw the strength from the belly, but at the same time maintain the right condition of the koshi. Then the air enters by itself and fills the upper belly. At the end of the inhalation the lower hara becomes strong, by itself, and one can then quite naturally and smoothly change over to exhaling. The change from inhaling to exhaling and vice-versa must be completely smooth. . . .

When all the muscles of the body attain their right balance, the region of the stomach becomes concave during exhalation and the lower belly curves slightly outward. . . .In this exercise inhalation is short, whereas exhalation is long since the hara is being reinforced. . . .

The strength filling the koshi should in fact be a strength which acts as if the upper part of the body did not exist at all. . . . The koshi carries the upper body with a strength striving upward from below. . . .This right posture, which permits the body to maintain its proper perpendicular position, is the only way of attaining that degree of form which demonstrates the unity of life beyond all dualism. One must escape from that imprisonment in the ego which causes cramp in various parts, and then a condition of egolessness will arise. But at the edge of the abyss life rushes in again. . . .

If the koshi is the most important region for acquiring right posture, one could say that the next most important part is the neck. . . .The lower jaw of many people drops forward in a slack way. . . .So the masters taught that one should keep the cervical vertebrae straight and put strength into the neck, in fact to pull the chin in so far that it hurts behind the ears. In the right posture the strength one puts into the koshi and the strength which pulls in the chin are closely connected. If one loses the strength of the koshi, the chin falls too far forward. . . If one tries only to pull the chin in without attention to the koshi and the pit of the stomach, the chest will involuntarily spring forward. When the chest protrudes, the belly muscles are drawn up and the whole musculature of the body is displaced. . . .One must create

from the hara the strength which keeps the neck in order. . . .
When the strength of the neck enters that of the tanden. . . the
head feels as if it were lightly floating no matter which way it
moves.[2] (Parenthesis mine.)

In Japanese, posture literally means the force in which the breath
stands. When breathing is concentrated at the tanden, each exhalation releases tension in the upper body and gathers the strength of
the body in the hara. This causes energy to radiate through the body
and perfect its form. A master wrote, "One breath after the other
with the whole body strength of the tanden—this is like a chisel
which gradually shapes up all the muscles fully, organically."

The limits to refining breathing and posture through training the
musculature depend on one's kinesthetic sensitivity. This sensitivity
can be extraordinarily heightened through sitting zazen, which elim-
inates the gross random movements normally masking and dissipat-
ing the energy needed to experience the subtler sensations of the
body. Patterns of tension can be traced from head to toe; the flow of
blood and energy can be experienced and harmonized with the pulsation of the Universe.

Itzhak Bentov, a developer of medical instruments, describes the
following dynamics between body motion, heartbeat, and breathing.
This is an example of one possible mechanism of creating a resonant rhythm in the body through breathing.

When the left ventricle of the heart ejects blood, the aorta,
being elastic, balloons out just beyond the valve and causes a
pressure pulse to travel down along the aorta. . . .When the
pulse reaches the bifurcation in the lower abdomen (which is
where the aorta forks in two to go into the legs), part of the
pressure pulse rebounds and starts travelling up the aorta. If in
the meantime the heart ejects more blood, and a new pressure
pulse is travelling down, these two pressure fronts will eventually collide somewhere along the aorta and produce an interfer-
ence pattern. This is. . . the reason for the irregular pattern of
(normal) body motion. . . .

However, when the breathing stops, it looks as if some communication has been set up between the heart and the bifurcation. Some kind of signal seems to travel from the bifurcation
to the heart, saying to it, "Heart, hold it. Hold your next pulse
until the echo from the bifurcation returns to you—only then
should you eject the next quantity of blood." When this happens,

and the echo and the pulse move out of the heart together, and they continue to move up and down in synchrony, then such a system is said to be in resonance. It causes the body to move harmoniously up and down about seven times a second, hence the nice, regular, large-amplitude sine-wave pattern. . . .Another characteristic of resonant behavior is that it requires for its sustenance a minimum amount of energy.[3]

Ultimately the resonant rhythm of the body can be entrained with the rhythm of the Universe when embryo breathing is attained.

In the high-tech environment of modern society, unless one does manual labor, a person is unlikely to satisfy the need for physical stimulation engrained by evolution. Most people must make an effort to integrate exercise into their lifestyle. When done according to the principles of breathing, posture, and awareness developed in the Ways, exercise leads to hara development, the cultivation of vital energy, and the transformation of personality. Any exercise can be practiced in this manner. One which is ideally suited as a daily practice because it is quiet and requires little space and no partner is T'ai Chi. It is a sophisticated Chinese martial art practiced through slow, graceful movements reflecting the natural flow of the Tao. Steven Kow, instructor of Tai Chi at Chozen-ji, lists the following as areas emphasized in the art:

1. Concentration of the mind.
2. Practice of the forms.
3. Control of internal breathing, coordinating the rhythm of breathing with the movements of the body.
4. Development of the tanden.
5. The attainment of Emptiness in which a person's small self merges with Tao.[4]

Circulating Energy

Well-being consists of the free flow of vital energy throughout the body and between the body and the universe. Circulating energy is the practice of dissolving the aberrations in the body which impair the flow of energy. This is the goal of Zen body therapy, a method of bodywork developed by Dub Leigh in consultation with Tanouye Roshi. Leigh is one of two people in the world who has been personally trained by Ida Rolf and Moshe Feldenkrais. He describes Zen body therapy as the manual manipulation of random patterns of vital energy. He writes:

After my training in structure by Ida Rolf and in function by Moshe Feldenkrais, the work with Tanouye Roshi at Chozen-ji was like a post-graduate course in energy and the meaning of life and death. It now seems clear that we are one with all the energy of the universe and we are truly one with whatever is.

Neither the structure, function, nor energy of the body can be changed without changing the others. All three are interpenetrating and need to be brought to the same level of alignment and balance.

The structure and function of the well-processed bodies turned out by Rolfing, Feldenkrais, and Zen therapy and training are quite different. Ida's processed bodies have a lift, a lightness that reminds me of a bullfighter. Moshe's processed bodies have more mobility and appear fluid in almost all configurations. Zen processed bodies are grounded. They seem almost unmovable by any outside force, yet they have a smooth gliding motion, and never seem to lose their groundness with the universe.

All of the above well-processed bodies house psyches that are much more emotionally mature and optimistic than the nonprocessed. They live mostly in enthusiasm, cheerfulness, interest and contentment. When appropriate, they can move down to hostility, anger, hate, resentment, fear and despair. Only rarely, under unusual conditions, will they drop down to grief, self-abasement or apathy. When they do, they bounce back fast. Failure, shame, or blame do not exist for a well-processed body. They do not "muck around" in any of the negative emotions. Most important is, that everyone's life gets better, "whether they like it or not" to quote Moshe. It happens just in the course of being processed. Ida called it the "free lunch."

Now when it comes to the psyches of the processed bodies, the difference is seen in the Zen-trained. The psyches of the Zen-trained are at a higher plane. Because it aims at transcending duality and becoming one with all that is, Zen body therapy includes one more dimension: preparing the body for its inevitable death. This process involves reaching into the person's subconscious and unconscious to allow the release of pent-up traumas, physical as well as emotional, which have generated aberrations in the body. These physical and emotional scars from past traumas impede a smooth transition of the vital energy into the hereafter. The psychophysical cleansing of Zen body therapy facilitates the orderly release of vital energy at the point of death.[5]

A person can facilitate the release of blocks through using visualization and breathing to generate and focus the energy needed to dissolve blocks in the body. The philosopher Chang Chung-yuan's account of Taoist breathing is informative:

> One has to send a genuine idea along with the movement of breathing. When inhaling, one lets the idea sink from the heart region down to the region of the kidney or the sea of breath. When exhaling, one brings the idea from the tip of the spine and back to the region of the heart. Thus one completes the lesser circulation. Actually, of course, the breath cannot travel through the spine and the abdomen, but the sending of the idea along the path of the lesser circulation is very like breathing along this pathway. Perhaps we may refer to this movement as a heat current that moves along the lesser circulation by one's idea. The same is true of the grand circulation; one leads the current by his idea from the tip of the spine all the way upward to the top of the head and from there one lets the current descend through the face and chest back to the abdomen. The ability to move this current by one's idea is acquired by training. After a short period of concentration one feels that one can easily send his idea to any chosen spot. . . .This genuine idea can only emerge from the state of no-thought, or nonbeing, which is neither a thought nor an idea in the conventional sense. It is an inner awareness of one's concentration on the centers (of energy in the body) and the movement along the paths of circulation.[6]

When one develops the ability to generate and direct the heat current, one can focus energy to dissolve blocks in the body from the inside out as Hakuin did in his practice of *naikan*. Combined with simple techniques from Zen body therapy, this forms an extremely effective method of releasing the natural, enlightened form of the body.

Communication

Because communication is the medium in which we live, it is generally overlooked as a skill which can be learned. Yet there are formal errors such as deletion, incongruence, generalization, redundancy, and intellectualization which are common and can be corrected. More fundamental, however, are values. When values are shallow, interpersonal interaction remains unfulfilling no matter what. But when the primary value is self-realization, then communication leads to contact that enriches all involved.

Swordfighting can serve as a paradigm for communication. In a swordfight two men armed with swords and concentration honed to the sharpest edge fight to the death. In swordsmanship, at first the feeling of mutual slaying, of taking the opponent's life even at the cost of one's own is stressed. But the highest level is communion and not confrontation. The master swordsman approaches the life and death encounter with the psychophysical attitude called "open on all sides." Undefensive with no attachments, he is completely relaxed and concentrated in the present time and space. Because he is centered, he is capable of infinite movement and therefore has no opening. He responds according to the patterns enfolded in the implicate order. When two masters meet, the result is mutual passing.

In the end interactions become finer and finer until sensing, interpreting, and responding occur naturally from a communion beyond words. Thus Takuan compared the first transmission of Zen to a swordfight:

> When one master crosses the point of his sword with another, and no longer thinks in terms of victory or defeat, we are reminded of the tradition of how Kasho Bodhisattva (the Second Indian Patriarch) smiled when Shakamuni Buddha held a flower between his finger as he preached.[7]

Odagiri Ichiun's account of his training with Hariya Sekiun, the founder of the school called, "The Sword of No Abiding Mind," illustrates Takuan's comment. Sekiun had mastered the technique of swordsmanship before training under Zen Master Kohaku.

> Sekiun ultimately came to this conclusion: none of the great professors of swordsmanship so far as he knew, including his own teacher Genshin and Genshin's teacher Kami-idzumi, could be called real masters of the art. For they utterly failed in understanding the fundamental principle of life; without it, however advanced their mastery of technique, they were all slaves to delusive thoughts, worth absolutely nothing. They could not go beyond these three alternatives: (1) to defeat the inferior enemy; (2) to be defeated by the superior one; and (3) with an equal, to end in mutual striking-down or killing (ai-uchi).
> Sekiun now employed himself in learning how to perfect the art of swordsmanship along the line of Heavenly Reason or Primary Nature in the state of as-it-is-ness. He was convinced that such a principle was applicable to the art. One day he had a great awakening. He discovered that there was no need in swordplay

to resort to the so-called technicality. When a man is enthroned in the seat of Heavenly Reason, he feels as if he were absolutely free and independent, and from this position he can cope most readily with all sorts of professional trickery. When Sekiun, my teacher, tried his discovery with his teacher Osgasawara Genshin, Sekiun easily defeated Genshin even though Genshin exhausted all his secret arts. It was like burning bamboo in the flames of an angry fire.

Sekiun was then already past sixty when I, Ichiun, twenty-eight years old, came to him as a pupil. During the five years of tutorship under Sekiun, I applied myself most earnestly and assiduously to the art of swordsmanship, which was now taught by the old master in the form newly synthesized with the principle and practice of Zen. When I thought I was finally ready to try my attainment with the master, I challenged him, and at each of the three contests we were engaged in, the outcome was what was called "*ai-nuke*" (mutual passing). . . .

Soon after this my teacher passed away, and I was left to myself. For the six following years I was in retirement, quietly contemplating Heavenly Reason, and I had no idea of propagating my newly acquired art. Instead I devoted myself to a life of introspection so that I forgot even to feel hunger and cold.

One significant fact I have to mention in connection with my contests with the master is that, after the third test, the master gave me a scroll containing words of testimony in which he fully recognized his disciple's realization of the principle of swordsmanship. The master then took out a rosary from his chest pocket, and, burning incense, turned toward me and bowed in the way the Buddhists generally do toward their object of reverence.

I really did not know what the master meant by this religious act. There is no doubt, however, that the master thereby paid to his young pupil the highest compliment one mortal could ever give another (Second parenthesis mine.)[8]

Training Retreats

The Japanese have six words for training, each signifying a deeper, more encompassing practice. The last is *shugyo*. Refining the self in *shugyo* is like forging a sword from iron ore. Fire, water, and iron are folded upon each other by the pounding of the hammer over and over again to create the cutting edge. If a person trains to acquire

enlightenment as an end, frustration is inevitable for the Way is end-less. But if one takes life as training, sees through both good and bad fortune as the effects of karma, and uses whatever comes for further development, then one enjoys life fully. As Dogen said, "Training is enlightenment, and enlightenment is training."

Training retreats are periods of intense, continuous training to recollect the awareness dissipated in ordinary life. Such concen-trated effort is needed to breakthrough ordinary sets and precon-ceived limitations. Training retreats revolve around the four basic practices and are based on the Zen *sesshin*. *Sesshin* literally means collecting the mind and is a time of uninterrupted training lasting about five days.

Though most of *sesshin* consists of zazen, detailed forms of behav-ior refined over centuries are enforced to foster alertness in every situation. Any activity can be made into practice, eating for example. Participants eat in two lines. Each has a set of five lacquered bowls fitting into each other and bundled in a cloth with chopsticks inserted at the top. The bowls must be unwrapped quickly and without noise while the Heart Sutra is being chanted. This is best done by flipping the bowls upside down and removing the largest first. Then depend-ing on whether it is breakfast, lunch, or dinner, different chants are recited as the food is served. The server extends both hands toward the person with palms up and left hand forward. The participant must place the correct bowl into the palm of the server's left hand without wasting any time, and yet the act should be graceful and unhurried. While being served, hands are held palm to palm in front of the chest. Enough is indicated by moving the right hand forward; a little more by rubbing the hands. Eating proceeds quickly. Every-thing edible must be eaten. Second and third servings are offered, and when the adjacent person is being served, bowls and chopsticks must be put down. There is reason and efficiency and the possibility of beauty and grace in all this, but the beginner feels so busy that there seems to be no time to eat. At the end of the meal, servers run wipecloths over the table scattering any bowls left on. Such detailed forms coupled with the demand for efficiency prevent a person from losing concentration.

Training retreats may not be as structured as sesshin and may be adapted according to individual needs, but like *sesshin* the purpose is to recollect awareness through concentrated, extended effort. It is to reestablish the psychophysical homeostasis needed for continued growth. Along with regular practice, intense periods of training are needed to breakthrough the limitations of the ego.

In Zen, Ten Ox-herding pictures depict adult maturation. In the first the oxherd searches vainly for the ox which represents his true Self. In the second he sees its traces, and in the third the ox itself. In the fourth he catches the ox, but it is wild. In the fifth he exerts himself to the utmost to tame it. In the sixth, playing a flute, he rides home on the back of the ox. In the seventh the ox is gone, and finally at home he sits serenely alone. In the eighth an empty circle represents the transcendence of dualism. In the ninth a natural landscape represents the transcendence of emptiness. In the tenth a smiling, fat man, bare-chested and bare-footed, enters the market place with bliss-bestowing hands. He radiates vital energy, and wherever he goes, samadhi prevails.

All Ways Are One
in the End

We have reached a point when human weaknesses and limitations must be addressed for society and culture to advance. More important than any technology is the development of the person. It is said that when the right person uses the wrong means, the wrong means work in the right way; but when the wrong person uses the right means, the right means work in the wrong way. All Ways are one in the end because effectiveness and creativity ultimately come from self-development. The end of all Ways is to live freely in samadhi.

It was Miyamoto Musashi who said, "All Ways are one in the end." He was peerless in fencing, and some of his works in painting, calligraphy, woodcarving, and metalwork are national treasures of Japan. Fittingly his book on swordsmanship, *The Book of Five Rings*, is currently being advertised as "the real art of Japanese management."

Miyamoto was born in 1584 into a low-ranking samurai family.[1] As a child he was quick, strong, and willful. He constantly played at fencing with the stick and quickly mastered all the techniques his father knew. At the age of thirteen he accepted the open challenge of a swordsman with a fine record of victories and killed him. At twenty-one he left his hometown for Kyoto and challenged the prestigious Yoshioka school of fencing. Instead of just dismissing Miyamoto as beneath him, the head of the school, Genzaemon, agreed to a bout with wooden swords at five in the morning. Genzaemon arrived on time, but two hours passed without Miyamoto appearing. Thinking that Miyamoto had fled, Genzaemon suppressed the urge to ridicule him and ordered his disciples to check Miyamoto's inn. When they returned, they reported, "Miyamoto was still sleeping. He was so impertinent that he said, 'I have overslept, but I will come soon. Please give my regards to your master.' " Genzaemon raged, but another two hours passed before Miyamoto came. Shouting angrily, Genzaemon immediately attacked. Miyamoto looked cool and composed. They crossed swords three times, and both were hit on the forehead. Suddenly Miyamoto launched his attack. Genzaemon could not withstand it and collapsed to the ground unconscious. His right arm had been shattered. Genzaemon subsequently entered the priesthood.

Genzaemon's younger brother Denshichiro then challenged Miyamoto to restore the family name. Denshichiro surpassed Genzaemon in fencing by far. Once again, despite his promise, Miyamoto was late, acting indifferently to time. As soon as the dual started, Miyamoto moved like lightning and fatally cut Denshichiro.

Miyamoto's fame spread while the Yoshiokas seethed for revenge. They decided to challenge Miyamoto to a duel in the name of Genzaemon's child Matashichiro and attack in unison when Miyamoto came. Knowing this, Miyamoto nevertheless accepted and allowed none of his followers to accompany him. The day of the duel dawned with Miyamoto at the site long before he was due. After examining the features of the land, Miyamoto took cover to observe developments. Surrounded by Yoshioka men, Matashichiro came into sight. They were armed with bows and spears as well as swords. Expecting Miyamoto to be late again, they relaxed, laid down their weapons, and stretched out. When they dropped their guard, Miyamoto jumped out and shouted, "I've been waiting long enough! Draw your sword!" Gathering speed he fatally slashed Matashichiro across the forehead. The Yoshioka followers were caught off guard and struck dumb. They had planned to surround Miyamoto and attack as a body. With sharp, quick strokes he forced those near him in a line and slew them in rapid succession. Just as the Yoshiokas grouped themselves to attack, Miyamoto abruptly turned and ran as fast as he could. Again bewildered, the Yoshiokas managed only to nick Miyamoto's sleeve with an arrow.

After this victory Miyamoto journeyed throughout Japan for eight years in search of opponents. He carried a list of nineteen points about self discipline, such as: "Never grieve on parting. Revere the gods and Buddha, but do not pray for anything. Do not possess a home of your own." During this period he fought about sixty duels, an average of more than one every two months.

His greatest opponent was Sasaki Ganryu. Sasaki was famed for a lightning fast counter stroke based on the movements of a swallow's tail in flight, and even the lord hosting Miyamoto felt that Sasaki would win. The duel was set for eight in the morning on an island. Sasaki arrived promptly, finely dressed and with an unconventionally long sword made by a famous smith. Miyamoto was once again very late. Officials found him still asleep. Despite their prodding, he woke leisurely, dawdled over breakfast, and carved an oar into a long wooden sword. Finally he boarded the boat, tied his kimono sleeves back with a sash, and laid down. As soon as the boat reached the island, Miyamoto jumped out and tied a towel for a headband.

Sasaki shouted, "Are you so afraid that you broke your promise to be here by eight?" Miyamoto ignored this and composedly, even jauntily, began to measure the distance to Sasaki. The waves lapped at his feet as Miyamoto steadily closed. Sasaki drew his long sword and threw the sheath on the beach. Miyamoto stopped, stared at Sasaki then at the sheath, and shook his head slightly in disbelief. He smiled scornfully and said, "Sasaki, you have sealed your doom." "Me? Defeated? Impossible!" responded Sasaki. "What victor on earth would abandon his sheath to the sea?" said Miyamoto.

Sasaki raised his sword high and slashed at the center of Miyamoto's forehead with a stroke as fast as light. It was full of confidence and power. But at the same time Miyamoto brought his sword down too. Miyamoto's headband was cut in two, but it was Sasaki who staggered to the ground. Miyamoto stepped forward when Sasaki suddenly lashed out from the ground as he regained his feet and cut Miyamoto's kimono. Miyamoto leaped in and dealt a fatal blow. Blood spurted from Sasaki's mouth as he died. Miyamoto stared at him, bowed towards the officials in charge, and then left. After the duel with Sasaki, Miyamoto returned to Kyoto where he opened his first fencing school and began to study other arts including calligraphy, tea ceremony, and painting. Eventually he created masterpieces which have been designated as national treasures of Japan.

He left Kyoto in 1614 to fight in two major civil battles and then resumed his wanderings. Several lords sought to retain him, but Miyamoto refused. During his time he perfected fencing with two swords and was convinced that no one could touch him. Once Miyamoto was challenged by a boastful swordsman who had a wooden

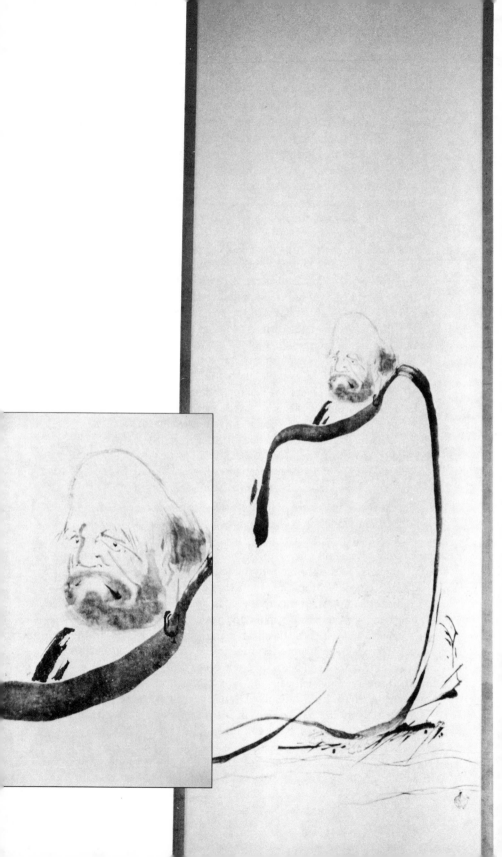

sword decorated with crimson streamers. Miyamoto ordered a page
to fetch a few grains of boiled rice and then placed one on his head.
The page stood bolt upright. As Miyamoto drew his sword and raised
it, all present held their breath. Miyamoto cut down without touch-
ing the child, but a close look revealed that the grain was cut in half.
Miyamoto repeated the same feat twice more. Then he glared at the
swordsman, "You and your ostentatious sword. How can you hope
to excel with that attitude!"

At the age of forty-eight Miyamoto travelled to Edo, which had
become the center of the shogunate. He wanted to challenge Yagyu
Munenori, who was the instructor to the Shogun and reputed to be
without equal. Miyamoto researched Munenori exhaustively and
concluded that he could defeat him. Two times, however, Miyamoto
inexplicably turned down opportunities to face him.

At the age of fifty-four Miyamoto left Edo to participate in quel-
ling a peasant rebellion. Following the end of the rebellion in 1638,
Miyamoto was persistently entreated by Lord Hosokawa to serve as
a retainer. For two years Hosokawa sent messengers every two or
three months till Miyamoto finally consented.

When Miyamoto arrived at the castle, he found the Hosokawa
retainers sitting lined in formal fashion in impeccable attire. Miyamoto surveyed them as he walked between them to the inner cham-
ber where he bowed and formally greeted Lord Hosokawa. Accepting
the greeting, Hosokawa good humoredly asked Miyamoto, "What do
you think of my retainers?" Miyamoto replied, "There are many
excellent samurai among them, but one has attracted my attention
far more than any other." Hosokawa was surprised and called his
retainers in one by one. Those of the highest rank entered first, but
Miyamoto did not single anyone out. Finally, smiling with slight
embarassment, Hosokawa said, "This method is becoming trouble-
some. Please go and bring the one you have in mind."

Miyamoto returned with Toko, a low-ranking, inconspicuous
samurai. Hosokawa looked quizzically at Miyamoto. Miyamoto
turned to Toko and said, "Your lord has ordered you to commit
seppuku. Go and prepare yourself." Without the slightest change of
expression, without hesitation or confusion, Toko bowed to his lord
and left to prepare himself. Miyamoto turned to Hosokawa and said,
"He is what you have seen." Hosokawa nodded. Miyamoto added,
"What an admirable samurai. He is prepared to accept death at any
moment."

Calling Toko back, Hosokawa asked Miyamoto what had drawn
his attention to him. Miyamoto said, "This one attracted me because

he surpassed all the others in alertness and sharpness of mind and body. Such thorough attentiveness is only possessed by those who have totally internalized the spirit of the samurai."

Miyamoto and Hosokawa became very close until the lord died several years later. Miyamoto would have liked to commit seppuku and follow him, but the practice had been outlawed. Moreover if Miyamoto who was only a guest retainer did this, others might be compelled to do the same. Miyamoto's health deteriorated suddenly, and he often lay sick in bed.

He retired to a mountain cave where he lived his last two years and composed *The Book of Five Rings* which has five parts: Earth, Water, Fire, Wind, and Emptiness. Miyamoto called his teachings the *Nitten Ichi* Way of Strategy. Nitten Ichi means two heavens as one. Excerpts from this book follow.

THE BOOK OF FIVE RINGS

When I reached thirty, I looked back on my past. The previous victories were not due to my having mastered strategy. Perhaps it was natural ability, or the order of Heaven, or that the strategy of other schools were inferior. After that I studied from morning till night searching for the principle, and came to realize the Way of strategy when I was fifty.

Since then I have lived without following any particular Way. With the virtue of strategy I practice many arts and abilities—all things with no teacher.[2]

This is the Way for men who want to learn my strategy:
1. Do not think dishonestly.
2. The Way is in training.
3. Become acquainted with every art.
4. Know the Ways of all professions.
5. Distinguish between gain and loss in worldly matters.
6. Develop intuitive judgement and understanding for everything.
7. Perceive those things which cannot be seen.
8. Pay attention even to trifles.
9. Do nothing which is of no use.

It is important to start by setting these broad principles in your heart. . . .If you do not look at things on a large scale, it will be difficult for you to master strategy. If you learn and attain this strategy, you will never lose even to twenty or thirty enemies. More than anything to start with you must set your heart on strategy and earnestly stick to the Way. You will come to be able to actually beat men in fights, and to be able to win with your eye. Also by training you will be able to freely control your own body, conquer men with your body, and with sufficient training you will be able to beat ten men with your spirit. . . .Moreover, in large scale strategy the superior man will manage many subordinates dextrously, bear himself correctly, govern the country and foster the people, thus preserving the ruler's discipline.[3]

The Nitten Ichi Way of Strategy is recorded in this the Book of Emptiness.

What is called the mind/spirit of Emptiness is where there is No Form, that which is unknowable. This is Emptiness.

People in the world look at things mistakenly and think that what they do not understand must be Emptiness. This is not True Emptiness. All this is delusion. . . .

Day and night polish the two-fold Mind and Spirit and sharpen the two-fold perception, intuition and sight. When there is not a bit of the clouds of delusion, then this is True Emptiness. . . .

Enact strategy broadly, correctly and openly. Then you will come to think of things in a wide sense, and taking Emptiness as the Way, you will see the Way as Emptiness. In Emptiness, there is virtue and no evil. There is wisdom, principle, and the Way.[4]

Notes

INTERPENETRATION,
THE BUDDHA'S ENLIGHTENMENT (pp. 1-13)

1 D.T. Suzuki, *What is Zen?* (New York: Harper and Row, 1972), p. 94.

2 Prabhavananda and C. Isherwood, *Shankara's Crest-Jewel of Discrimination* (New York: New American Library, 1970), pp. 92-93.

3 Aldous Huxley, *The Perennial Philosophy* (New York: Harper and Row, 1970), p. 57.

4 *Ibid.*, p. 5.

5 Kenneth Wilber, *Up from Eden* (New York: Anchor Press, 1981), p. 6.

6 Kenneth Wilber, *The Spectrum of Consciousness* (Wheaton: Theosophical Publishing House, 1977), p. 34.

7 *Ibid.*, p. 38.

8 *Ibid.*, p. 54.

9 Wilber, 1981, p. 4.

10 David Bohm, *Wholeness and the Implicate Order* (London: Routledge and Kegan Paul, 1980), pp. 179-184.

11 *Ibid.*, pp. 187-189.

12 D.T. Suzuki, *Essays in Zen Buddhism, First Series* (New York: Grove Press, 1961), p. 176.

13 Zenkei Shibayama, *Zen Comments on the Mumonkan*, tr. S. Kudo (New York: Harper and Row, 1974), p. 350.

14 Trevor Leggett, *A First Zen Reader* (Rutland: Charles E. Tuttle, 1960), p. 64.

15 Sogen Omori, *Sanzen Nyumon* (Unpublished in English).

16 Fritjof Capra, *The Turning Point* (New York: Bantam Books, 1983), pp. 359-360.

17 Carl Jung, *Psychological Reflections*, ed. J. Jacobi and R.F.C. Hull (Princeton University Press, 1974), pp. 42-43.

18 Carl Jung, *Synchronicity*, tr. R.F.C. Hull (Princeton: Princeton University Press, 1973), pp. 109-110.

19 Abraham Maslow, *Toward a Psychology of Being* (New York: Van Nostrand Reinhold, 1968), pp. iii-iv.

20 Richard Mann, *The Light of Consciousness* (Albany: State University of New York Press, 1984), pp. 119-120.

21 Jung, 1974, p. 37.

BODHIDHARMA (pp. 19-24)

1 Chang Chung-yuan, *Tao: A New Way of Thinking* (New York: Harper and Row, 1975), p. 93.

2 D.T. Suzuki, *Essays in Zen Buddhism, First Series* (New York: Grove Press, 1961), p. 173.

3 Paraphrased from: Suzuki, 1961, p. 189.

4 This combines Zenkei Shibayama, *Zen Comments on the Mumonkan*, tr. S. Kudo (New York: Harper and Row, 1974), p. 287 and Suzuki, 1961, p. 191. Some accounts say that Hui-ke's arm was actually cut off by bandits.

5 Suzuki, 1961, pp. 185-186.

6 Suzuki, 1961, p. 186.

7 D.T. Suzuki, *Manual of Zen Buddhism* (New York: Grove Press, 1960), pp. 73-76.

HUI-NENG TA-CHIEN (pp. 25-30)

1 The following account of Hui-neng's life is based primarily on Zenkei Shibayama, *Zen Comments on the Mumonkan*, tr. S. Kudo (New York: Harper and Row, 1974), pp. 166-174.

2 D.T. Suzuki, *The Zen Doctrine of No Mind* (New York: Samuel Weiser, 1973), p. 24.

3 D.T. Suzuki, *Essays in Zen Buddhism, First Series* (New York: Grove Press, 1961), pp. 219-220.

4 Suzuki, 1973, p. 33.

5 *Ibid.*

6 *Ibid.*, p. 40.

7 *Ibid.*, p. 36.

8 D.T. Suzuki, *Essays in Zen Buddhism, Third Series* (New York: Samuel Weiser, 1976), pp. 35-36.

9 *Ibid.*, p. 54.

LIN-CHI I-HSUAN (pp. 31-38)

1 D.T. Suzuki, *Essays in Zen Buddhism, Second Series* (New York: Samuel Weiser, 1976), p. 79.

2 Zenkei Shibayama, *Zen Comments on the Mumonkan* (New York: Harper and Row, 1974), p. 215.

3 D.T. Suzuki, *Essays in Zen Buddhism, First Series* (New York: Grove Press, 1961), p. 240.

4 *Ibid*, pp. 247-248.

5 *Ibid*, p. 315.

6 Sogen Omori, *Sanzen Nyumon* (Unpublished in English).

7 Isshu Miura and Ruth Sasaki, *Zen Dust* (New York: Harcourt, Brace, and World, 1966), p. 231.

8 Erich Fromm, et al., *Zen Buddhism and Psychoanalysis* (New York: Harper and row, 1970), p. 29.

9 Ruth Sasaki, *The Record of Lin-chi* (Kyoto: Institute for Zen Studies, 1975), pp. 51-52.

10 *Ibid.*, p. 53.

11 *Ibid.*, p. 54.

12 *Ibid.*

13 *Ibid.*, p. 56.

14 *Ibid.*, p. 62.

15 Trevor Leggett, *The Tiger's Cave* (London: Routledge and Kegan Paul, 1977), pp. 183-185.

16 *Ibid.*, pp. 183-184.

17 *Ibid.*, pp. 191-192.

18 Sasaki, 1975, pp. 11-12.

19 *Ibid.*, pp. 16-18.

HAKUIN EKAKU (pp. 39-52)

1 Isshu Miura and Ruth Sasaki, *Zen Dust* (New York: Harcourt, Brace, and World, 1966), p. 206.

2 Trevor Leggett, *The Tiger's Cave* (London: Routledge and Kegan Paul, 1977), p. 162.

3 Miura and Sasaki, 1966, p. 233.

4 D.T. Suzuki, *What is Zen?* (New York: Harper and Row, 1972), p. 78.

5 D.T. Suzuki, *Manual of Zen Buddhism* (New York: Grove Press, 1960), p. 148.

6 Miura and Sasaki, 1966, pp. 325-326.

7 Unpublished literature of Chozen-ji.

8   Philip Yampolsky, *The Zen Master Hakuin* (New York: Columbia University Press, 1971), p. 67.

9   Miura and Sasaki, 1966., p. 215.

10   English accounts contradict each other on various details of Hakuin's life. The following account has been drawn primarily from Yampolsky, 1971, pp. 117-122 and Leggett, 1977, pp. 129-133.

11   Yampolsky, 1971, p. 118.

12   Leggett, 1977, p. 142.

13   *Ibid.*, p. 150.

14   Yampolsky, 1971, p. 42.

15   Leggett, 1977, pp. 153-154.

16   *Ibid.*, p. 132.

17   Yampolsky, 1971, p. 121.

18   Trevor Leggett, *A First Zen Reader* (Rutland: Charles Tuttle, 1972), p. 178.

19   Yampolsky, 1971, p. 32.

20   *Ibid.*, p. 45.

21   *Ibid.*, p. 59.

22   *Ibid.*, p. 65.

23   *Ibid.*, p. 69.

24   *Ibid.*, p. 145.

25   This translation combines Leggett, 1972, pp. 67-68 and Zenkei Shibayama, *A Flower Does Not Talk*, tr. S. Kudo (Rutland: Charles Tuttle, 1975), pp. 65-67.

OMORI SOGEN (pp. 53-63)

1   Sogen Omori, *Sanzen Nyumon* (Unpublished in English).

2   Tsunetomo Yamamoto, *Hagakure*, tr. W. Wilson (Tokyo: Kodansha International, 1980), pp. 17-18.

3   Sogen Omori, *"Ken to Zen"*, *Chozen*, n. 6, May 1975, p. 10.

4   Omori, *Sanzen Nyumon*.

5   Trevor Leggett, *Zen and the Ways* (Boulder: Shambhala Publications, 1978), p. 207.

6   Paraphrased from D.T. Suzuki, *Zen and Japanese Culture* (Princeton: Princeton University Press, 1973), pp. 195-196.

7   J.K. Kadowaki, *Zen and the Bible* (London: Routledge and Kegan Paul, 1980), pp. 78-79.

TANOUYE TENSHIN (pp. 65-76)

1 "Yagyu Munenori", *The East*, v. XII, n. 3, p. 61.

2 "Yagyu Munenori", *The East*, v. XII, n. 4, pp. 44-45.

3 Paraphrased from D.T. Suzuki, *Zen and Japanese Culture* (Princeton: Princeton University Press, 1973), pp. 212-213.

4 *Ibid.*, p. 200.

5 Trevor Leggett, *The Tiger's Cave* (London: Routledge and Kegan Paul, 1977), pp. 159-160.

THE WAY: A PHILOSOPHY OF LIFE (pp. 79-90)

1 D.T. Suzuki, *Zen and Japanese Culture* (Princeton: Princeton University Press, 1973), p. 79.

2 Phillip Yampolsky, *The Zen Master Hakuin* (New York: Columbia University Press, 1971), p. 54.

3 Karlfried von Durckheim, *Hara* (London: George Allen and Unwin, 1971), pp. 205-207.

4 Chang Chung-yuan, *Creativity and Taoism* (New York: Harper and Row, 1963), p. 135.

5 Thomas Merton, *The Way of Chuang-tzu* (New York: New Directions, 1969), pp. 45-47.

6 Chang Chung-yuan, *Tao: A New Way of Thinking* (New York: Harper and Row, 1975), p. 131.

7 Eugen Herrigel, *Zen in the Art of Archery* (New York: Pantheon Books, 1964), pp. 82-85.

8 Suzuki, 1973, pp. 142-143.

9 Paraphrased from Suzuki, 1973, pp. 428-432.

THE TRANSCENDENT UNCONSCIOUS AND THE TRUE SELF (pp. 91-98)

1 D.T. Suzuki, *Essays in Zen Buddhism, Third Series* (New York: Samuel Weiser, 1976), p. 74.

2 D.T. Suzuki, *Studies in the Lankavatara Sutra* (London: Routledge and Kegan Paul, 1975), p. 184.

3 *Ibid.*, pp. 191-192.

4 *Ibid.*, p. 201. In this passage Suzuki went on to identify the ultimate abiding place as the storehouse unconscious and wisdom as "a knowledge that is not of particularization and discrimination,. . . one of direct

experience in which the storehouse unconscious reveals itself in its original purity and not in its distorted and defiled forms as it ordinarily does to the senses." In the next quotation, however, he clearly identifies the ultimate abiding place as the transcendent unconscious. This distinction is consistent with that of Paramartha of the Yogacara School.

5 Erich Fromm, et. al, *Zen Buddhism and Psychoanalysis* (New York: Harper and Row, 1960), pp. 55-56.

6 *Japanese-English Buddhist Dictionary* (Tokyo: Daito Shuppansha, 1979), pp. 273-274.

7 Suzuki, 1975, pp. 197-198.

8 Trevor Leggett, *Zen and the Ways* (Boulder: Shambhala, 1978), p. 141.

9 D.T. Suzuki, *Zen in Japanese Culture* (Princeton University Press, 1973), pp. 224-225.

10 D.T. Suzuki, "Reason and Intuition in Buddhist Philosophy," *The Japanese Mind*, ed. C. Moore (Honolulu: University Press of Hawaii, 1975), p. 96.

11 Karlfried von Durckheim, *The Japanese Cult of Tranquility* (New York: Samuel Weiser, 1974), pp. 89-90.

12 Leggett, 1978, pp. 207-208.

CREATIVE PROBLEM SOLVING (pp. 99-118)

1 Zenkei Shibayama, *Zen Comments on the Mumonkan* (New York: Harper and Row, 1974), p. 140.

2 Paraphrased from: Trevor Leggett, *Zen and the Ways* (Boulder: Shambhala, 1978), pp. 222-225.

3 Jay Haley, *Uncommon Therapy* (New York: W.W. Norton, 1973), pp. 197-198.

4 Nick Cummings, *Biodyne Manual* (Unpublished).

5 Milton Erickson and Ernest Rossi, "Autohypnotic Experiences of Milton Erickson," *American Journal of Clinical Hypnosis*, 20, (1977), p. 37.

6 *Ibid.*, pp. 38-39.

7 Richard Bandler and John Grinder, *Patterns of the Hypnotic Techniques of Milton Erickson, M.D., V. I* (Cupertino: Meta Publications, 1975), pp. vii-viii.

8 Jay Haley, *Advanced Techniques of Hypnosis and Therapy* (New York: Grune and Stratton, 1967), p. 2.

9 Sidney Rosen, *My Voice Will Go with You* (New York: W.W. Norton, 1982), pp. 167-169.

10 Haley, 1973, pp. 310-313.

11 Milton Erickson, et. al., *Hypnotic Realities* (New York: Irvington Publishers, 1976), p. 9.

12 Erickson and Rossi, 1977, p. 44.

13 *Ibid.*, p. 43.

MIND-BODY TRAINING (pp. 119-138)

1 Omori Sogen, *Sanzen Nyumon* (Unpublished in English.)

2 Karlfried von Durckheim, *Hara* (London: George Allen and Unwin, 1971), pp. 192-198.

3 Itzhak Bentov, *Stalking the Wild Pendulum* (New York: Bantam Books, 1979), pp. 34-36.

4 Steven Kow, *Tai Chi Chuan* (Honolulu: Chozen-ji, 1980), p. 4.

5 Dub Leigh, "Zen Physical Therapy" (Unpublished.)

6 Chang Chung-yuan, *Creativity and Taoism* (New York: Harper and Row, 1963), pp. 155-156.

7 Karlfried Durckheim, *The Japanese Cult of Tranquility* (New York: Samuel Weiser, 1974), p. 91.

8 D.T. Suzuki, *Zen and Japanese Culture* (Princeton: University of Princeton Press, 1973), pp. 171-173.

ALL WAYS ARE ONE IN THE END (pp. 139-146)

1 The following account is based on "Miyamoto Musashi," *The East*, v. XI, nos. 7, 8, and 9, 1975.

2 Miyamoto Musashi, *A Book of Five Rings*, tr. V. Harris (New York: The Overlook Press, 1974), p. 35.

3 *Ibid.*, pp. 49-50.

4 Tanouye Tenshin, (Unpublished translation.)

Bibliography

Bandler, Richard, and Grinder, John. *Patterns of the Hypnotic Techniques of Milton H. Erickson, I.* Cupertino: Meta Publications, 1975.

Bentov, Itzhak. *Stalking the Wild Pendulum.* New York: Bantam Books, 1977.

Bohm, David. *Wholeness and the Implicate Order.* London: Routledge and Kegan Paul, 1980.

Capra, Fritjof. *The Turning Point.* New York: Bantam Books, 1983.

Cummings, Nick. *Biodyne Training Manual.* Unpublished.

Chung-yuan, Chang. *Creativity and Taoism.* New York: Harper and Row, 1970.

———. *Tao: A New Way of Thinking.* New York: Harper and Row, 1975.

Durckheim, Karlfried. *Hara.* London: George Allen and Unwin, 1971.

———. *The Japanese Cult of Tranquility.* New York: Samuel Weiser, 1974.

Erickson, Milton, Rossi, Ernest, and Rossi, Sheila. *Hypnotic Realities.* New York: Halstead Press, 1976.

Erickson, Milton and Rossi, Ernest. "Autohypnotic Experiences of Milton Erickson," *American Journal of Clinical Hypnosis,* 20, (1977).

———. *Hypnotherapy.* New York: Halstead Press, 1979.

Fromm, Erich, Suzuki, Daisetz, and DeMartino, Richard. *Zen Buddhism and Psychoanalysis.* New York: Harper and Row, 1970.

Haley, Jay (ed.) *Advanced Techniques of Hypnosis and Therapy.* New York: Grune and Stratton, 1967.

———. *Uncommon Therapy.* New York: W.W. Norton, 1973.

Herrigel, Eugen. *Zen in the Art of Archery.* New York: Pantheon Books, 1964.

Huxley, Aldous. *The Perennial Philosophy.* New York: Harper and Row, 1970.

154

Jung, Carl. *Synchronicity*. tr. R.F.C. Hull. Princeton: Princeton University Press, 1973.

_____. *Psychological Reflections*. ed. J. Jacobi. Princeton: Princeton University Press, 1974.

Kadowaki, J.K. *Zen and the Bible*. tr. J. Rieck. London: Routledge and Kegan Paul, 1980.

Kow, Steven. *Tai Chi Chuan*. Honolulu: Chozen-ji, 1980.

Leggett, Trevor. *A First Zen Reader*. Rutland: Charles Tuttle, 1972.

_____. *The Tiger's Cave*. London: Routledge and Kegan Paul, 1977.

_____. *Zen and the Ways*. Boulder: Shambhala, 1978.

Mann, Richard. *The Light of Consciousness*. Albany: State University Press of New York, 1984.

Maslow, Abraham. *Toward a Psychology of Being*. New York: Van Nostrand Reinhold, 1968.

Merton, Thomas. *The Way of Chuang-tzu*. New York: New Directions, 1969.

Miura, Isshu and Sasaki, Ruth. *Zen Dust*. New York: Harcourt, Brace, and World, 1966.

Miyamoto, Musashi, *The Book of Five Rings*. tr. V. Harris. Woodstock: The Overlook Press, 1974.

"Miyamoto Musashi," *The East*, v. XI, nos. 7, 8, 9, (1975).

Omori, Sogan. *Sanzen Nyumon*. Unpublished.

_____. *"Zen to Budo," Chozen*, n. 6 (1975).

Prabhavananda and Isherwood, Christopher. *Shankara's Crest Jewel of Discrimination*. New York: New American Library, 1970.

Sasaki, Ruth. *The Record of Lin-chi*. Kyoto: Institute for Zen Studies, 1975.

Shibayama, Zenkei. *A Flower Does Not Talk*. Tr. S. Kudo. Rutland: Charles Tuttle, 1970.

_____. *Zen Comments on the Mumonkan*. Tr. S. Kudo. New York: Harper and Row, 1974.

Suzuki, Daisetz. *Manual of Zen Buddhism*. New York: Grove Press, 1960.

_____. *Essays in Zen Buddhism, First Series*. New York: Grove Press, 1961.

_____. *What is Zen?*. New York: Harper and Row, 1972.

_____. *The Zen Doctrine of No Mind*. New York: Samuel Weiser, 1973.

_____. *Zen and Japanese Culture*. Princeton: Princeton University Press, 1973.

_____. "Reason and Intuition in Buddhist Philosophy." *The Japanese Mind*. Ed. C. Moore. Honolulu: University Press of Hawaii, 1975.

_____. *Studies in the Lankavatara Sutra*. London: Routledge and Kegan Paul, 1975.

————. *Essays in Zen Buddhism, Second Series.* New York: Samuel Weiser, 1976.

————. *Essays in Zen Buddhism, Third Series.* New York: Samuel Weiser, 1976.

Werner, Arnold, et. al. *A Psychiatric Glossary.* Washington, D.C., 1980.

Wilber, Kenneth. *The Spectrum of Consciousness.* Wheaton: Theosophical Publishing House, 1977.

————. *The Atman Project.* Wheaton: Theosophical Publishing House, 1980.

————. *Up from Eden.* New York: Anchor Press, 1981.

"Yagyu Munenori," *The East,* v. XII, nos. 3, 4, (1976).

Yamamoto, Tsunetomo. *Hagakure.* New York: Kodansha International, 1979.

Yampolsky, Philip. *The Zen Master Hakuin.* New York: Columbia University Press, 1971.

Index